31 DAYS (NIGHTS)

Memoir of Living Black in America

Reginald D. Jarrell

Blue Cedar Press
Wichita, Kansas

31 Days (Nights): Memoir of Living Black in America
Copyright © 2022 by Reginald D. Jarrell
All rights reserved. No part of this book may be reproduced in any form or by any electronic or mechanical means, including information storage and retrieval systems, without permission in writing from the publisher except for brief quotations quoted in critical articles and reviews. Inquiries should be addressed to:

Blue Cedar Press
PO Box 48715
Wichita, KS 67201

Visit the Blue Cedar Press website: www.bluecedarpress.com
10 9 8 7 6 5 4 3 2 1
First edition February 2022
ISBN: 978-1-7369112-7-3 (paper)
ISBN: 978-1-7369112-8-0 (ebook)

Cover design by Gina J. Lewis
Interior design by Gina Laiso, Integrita Productions
Editors Laura Tillem and Gretchen Eick

Library of Congress Control Number: 2022930901

Printed in the United States of America at IngramSpark and Amazon.

Dedication

For my ancestors, whose faces, names and lives I long to know. For my children, their children, and those to come who will only know my name. With love across eternity.

Contents

Note on Historical Context.. 7
Introduction.. 9
Day 1   Beginnings: 1960s-70s (Wichita, Kansas) 13
Day 2   The "N" Word:1960s (Muskogee, Oklahoma)........................ 19
Day 3   "Special Visitors" and Sunday Church: 1960s (Wichita)..... 21
Day 4   Aunt's Voice: 1960s (Wichita) 25
Day 5   Names: Sticks and Stones:1969-72 (Wichita)....................... 27
Day 6   Mrs. Reed/Mayberry Hall Monitor: 1969-72 (Wichita)........ 33
Day 7   Victory: Mr. Student Council President: 1971-72 (Wichita)..... 37
Day 8   West High Senior/Football: 1974-75 (Wichita)..................... 39
Day 9   Racial Profiling – DWB/First Time: 1974-75 (Wichita) 45
Day 10 A.U. and the "N" Word: 1977-78 (Washington, D.C.)......... 47
Day 11 Two Women and A.U.: 1977-78 (Washington, D.C.)........... 49
Day 12 Broadcasting /KAKE: 1978 (Wichita)..................................... 53
Day 13 Jack Shelley, Iowa State and WOI-TV: 1979-80 (Ames/Des Moines) 57
Day 14 Apartment Search: 1980 (Des Moines) 61
Day 15 S.U.N.O. and African Students: 1983-84 (New Orleans)........ 65
Day 16 The Parade: 1988-90 (Quad Cities) 69
Day 17 Stranger, Coach, Mentor, Friend–Jerry Goodmon, Sr: 1970-2022 (Wichita) 73
Day 18 The Judge: 1987-88 (Rock Island, Illinois)............................. 77
Day 19 Walking Diamond: 1988-91 (Davenport, Iowa) 79
Day 20 Prairie State – Mr. Man: 1990-92 (Rock Island, Illinois) 85
Day 21 The College President: 1997-98 (Quad Cities) 89
Day 22 Obama Wins: 2008 (Berkeley, California)............................. 95
Day 23 Invisible at the Buffet: 2012-20 (Wichita).............................. 97
Day 24 No Discount on Grace or Store Kindness: 2012-Current (Wichita) 99
Day 25 Mr. Walmart Greeter: 2012-20 (Wichita)............................. 103
Day 26 Oil Price Check and Bias: 2012-20 (Wichita) 105
Day 27 Voting Rights: 2012-Current (Wichita)................................. 109
Day 28 Utility Poles: 2012-Current (Wichita)................................... 111
Day 29 Death of a Friendship: 2012-Current (Wichita) 113
Day 30 Reading & Places: Travel Real and Imagined: 2012–Current (Wichita) 117
Day 31 Hope: 2012-Current (Wichita).. 119
About the Author...122

Note on Historical Context

This is a memoir of the last fifty years by a black man who earned four graduate degrees—Masters of Communications and Religion, a law degree, and a doctorate of ministry. Reginald D. Jarrell's story is unique, and it is also representative. Jarrell tells readers some of what he experienced living through a period of U.S. history that saw profound social and economic changes.

While the civil rights movement of the 1950s and 1960s brought federal protection for voting rights and access to public accommodations, education, and jobs, the 1970s saw U.S. corporations begin to export their manufacturing jobs abroad. This export of jobs to countries whose labor could be hired for a fraction of what the corporations had to pay U.S. workers, meant fewer manufacturing jobs in the U.S. This led to an unprecedented decline of the middle class.

Beginning with the 1972 presidential election campaign's "southern strategy," the Republican Party began seeking support from southern whites, resulting in a political realignment that produced a Solid South that was solidly Republican rather than Democrat. Republicans, the party of Lincoln, became the party that courted white supremacists. Republicans also dominated another region, where Reggie Jarrell was raised and raised his family — the Midwest.

During this time the explosion of internet technology — laptops, tablets, cell phones, etc. — affected the communications industry profoundly. The internet came to dominate people's access to news, and newspapers declined dramatically. That meant jobs in journalism grew more and more scarce to get and to hold onto.

Deregulation was popular in both political parties and the more deregulation, the more wealth in the U.S. was concentrated in the richest 1% of Americans; 20-25% of American children did not have enough to eat. The U.S. became a nation with two kinds of work predominating — service industry jobs and high tech jobs. The former often produced below poverty wages for full time work. The solution, young Americans were told, was to go to college.

A university education was accessible to those who could pay and to those willing to borrow. Student loans rose as the cost of post-secondary education rose dramatically. Students who graduated might think they'd be able to find well paying jobs, but the debt they accumulated grew and followed them like Pig Pen's cloud, with interest growing and growing. The impact was most devastating for first generation students whose families had been unable to accumulate wealth. It was not a problem for the children of the 1%.

These shifts in American life were hard enough if you were "white" — of European descent. If you were "black" or "brown," the institutionalized racism embedded in the United States for 400 years concentrated the impact of these factors, complicating your life and constricting your finances.

31 Days (Nights) tells how the factors constricting life for ordinary Americans like him played out in Jarrell's life. It tells a story of determination to make it, to thrive in this nation through hard work, self discipline, education, and keeping on. Jarrell's vision is honest; no group escapes his observations. He has written a powerful, moving memoir that is of his life and also of the United States of America.

Blue Cedar Press
Wichita, Kansas
February 12, 2022

Introduction
Setting the Stage

You can't judge a book by its cover, but so many people do. It happens so often. It can start early when we are children. And it happens to most people.

It isn't just that you like chocolate ice cream and I like vanilla. Or vice versa. That is bias or preference. Preferences, appear to be inherent. Prejudice is learned behavior. Prejudging something, or somebody and behaving toward them in ways that dismiss them because of preconceived notions.

When prejudice is acted out, people are damaged. When such mistreatment is applied broadly to particular groups of people because of their appearance, their color, attributes they cannot alter, it is called systemic racism.

Systemic and institutional racism, subtle and deeply ingrained throughout society, is invisible to many. Far too often it passes undetected and therefore goes unchallenged. But the short and long term effects can be tragic and devastating. Then there is the kind of prejudice that causes people to feel free to judge or ignore those they may not like. For example, while some people keep snakes as pets, other folk simply do not like snakes, period.

And some people just don't "like" you. For whatever reason. Or little to no reason.

You are Black/black, or brown or yellow... and they don't like it. You are too tall where they have to stand in your shadow or too short where they feel you block their glory. They don't like your cute button nose or your large expansive ears.

They don't like your big stoic brown eyes, your sparkling green eyes, your wide toothy grin. Yes, that's it! That gleaming, encouraging smile of yours just sends shivers down their very soul. They don't like the happiness and joy that you have. They don't experience the peace and satisfaction that you have. Or they don't like the twang in your voice, your high pitched laughter, your smooth, soulful, deep baritone voice, your.....

Your sure, confident strut is offensive and they smolder at how your effortless, prideful stride seems to glide.

They don't like you for a variety of reasons. Or no reason at all. Just because you exist. They don't know you and if they did, it wouldn't make any difference. They don't care to know you.

However, it's not really about you. It's about them, all about them. It's their world, or so they would like to believe, and they see you as intruding.

Sucking up their air.

Occupying their space.

Taking up their time.

As if they are God.

And that doesn't matter.

Throughout time people have excused, justified and rationalized discriminatory and hurtful actions in the name of, or in spite of, God. *31 Days (Nights)* is a snapshot of my journey, maneuvering around obstacles of bias and barriers of prejudice. Sometimes falling, sometimes failing, sometimes lost yet still surviving.

Sometimes savoring the joyful exhilaration of not just success but sweet victory.

Victory over bias? Over prejudice?

Oh yes, sometimes. Even if triumphs appear small and insignificant, they are not.

Every victory is a step on the ladder to stronger self-esteem, self-worth, self-satisfaction.

Because you have to take the victory whenever you can get it, wherever you can find it. However it comes.

And there is victory in surviving.

31 Days (Nights) provides instances where some have closed their eyes to the humanity of others. They have locked up, locked out and locked in their integrity in dungeons of arrogance and conceit and attempted to throw away the key. Note: attempted.

Yet someone, something comes along and keeps ringing the bells of freedom and justice and liberation and peace.

And someone shines the light of kindness and you discover, and rediscover, love.

For a moment and that's all it takes to catch a breath to continue on the journey.

Thus *31 Days (Nights)* includes some folk who ignored or erased imposed societal boundaries of race, culture, ethnicity and escaped the destructive traps of bias, prejudice and discrimination, who showed indelible marks of compassion, generosity and kindness. I have included other folk whose lightening sparks of encouragement and inspiration illuminated for me widespread, explosive, life sustaining hope.

31 Days (Nights) is symbolic as there are 31 days in some months. The beaming light of day versus the stillness, quietness of the dark night. Within the context of 31 Day (Nights) darkness is symbolic of the poison of racism, bias and prejudice.

31 Days (Nights) is my story of people and incidents I have experienced living black in America. My experiences within the framework of racism. Some experiences cross cultural, class, socioeconomic, religious, and other lines. I grew up in the Midwest, in a caring family and church played a major role in my life. I went on to earn degrees in communications, law, religion, and to work in the professions--as a television and newspaper journalist, tenured professor, attorney, and preacher. I also sold shoes and worked as a janitor and now teach at a university.

Please note, being a former television news reporter, some of my essays are written in a breezy, conversational style with short sentences reminiscent of a dialogue between family members. That is what we are, members of the same family, humankind, in *31 Days (Nights)*.

Welcome to my journey.

Day 1
Beginnings: 1960s-70's (Wichita, Kansas)

Imagine a symphony of children's laughter sifting through the neighborhood of well maintained, single family, middle-class homes with green grass and neatly manicured lawns. The omnipresent gaze of adult eyes watch ever vigilant over youngsters oblivious to the trials of society.

Everybody knew everyone on the block. Kids knew the nice and friendly folk, and the grumpy grouches who dared kids to not only stay off the grass but also to "stay off my driveway" when riding bikes. Miss Pauline and her teenage son lived next door, Mr. Russell's family was across the street on the corner and Mrs. B. resided up the street.

Growing up in a middle-class, two-parent home in a predominantly African American neighborhood in a middle-sized, predominantly Caucasian mid-western city, Wichita, Kansas, in the 1960s, I lived a sheltered life. We were "colored," "Negro," then "black" in those days.

Life revolved around family, the extended family, and the neighborhood. Everyone basically looked like me (although in varying shades from high yellow to dark brown.

Exposure to other folks who didn't look like us was rare and admittedly there was a time I wasn't sure what a "white" or Caucasian person looked like. I actually mistook light-skinned, yellow or tan black folk for being white. Honestly didn't know.

Was a patient of the kind Dr. W., who was Caucasian, but I didn't know it. I went to a rough, heavy-handed dentist but I didn't realize he was black. They were just people with very distinct personalities.

I remember watching television and seeing some of the Disney cartoon characters that portrayed dark, actually black-skinned peoples. For example, Africans portrayed with grossly exaggerated features: long, thin arms and legs, big buck eyes, large lips and white bones through their broad noses chasing after the innocent

Caucasian hunter/victim through the jungles. Clearly, blatantly racist. Dehumanizing. Savages and cannibals. On television screens. Yes I noticed but didn't realize those were portrayals of my ancestors.

Also, there were very dark-skinned, lazy, slothful actors, speaking in the slow, meandering drawl of a Stepin Fetchin styled cartoon caricature. And the large, dark-skinned, ever joyful mammy.

These were symbols of me. Of course, that's not how I saw myself.

I loved going to the movies. Those times in darkened movie theatres where I could escape to another world, another time, even another life were always positive experiences. Yet in many of those films there were no black folk. And if there were, they were minor characters such as servants, butlers, and maids.

Wonderful memories of 1960s Saturday mornings spent at the Nomar movie theater seeing special children's films. My folks would drop me off and I'd head up front, as close to the screen as possible. There was always a theatre full of children, I don't remember any adults, but I don't ever remember seeing anyone else who looked like me. Never. From what I could see and remember, I was the only one. I always went alone, never thought to ask if a friend could go with me. Regardless, no one ever bothered me. Ever. If someone said something, I never heard it. I never felt harassed or even stared at. No problems, ever. In the midst of all these other children I realized they looked different from me. I just didn't realize they were Caucasian or as some say, white.

Then there was Ingalls elementary, the neighborhood school only about four short blocks away, a straight shot east on 11th street. Oh was I excited to go there! But I also remember feeling anxious about the unknown. Didn't know what to expect but I looked forward to being in kindergarten.

The modern styled school was predominantly black with an integrated professional staff. The principal, Clyde Phillips, was black and always professionally dressed in a stylish coat, crisply ironed white shirt and tie. And my very first teacher put me at ease.

Miss (or Mrs. Westfall had short blonde hair, was middle aged and Caucasian, I just didn't know it at the time. What I did know was that she was a nice, considerate lady who made us feel comfortable, relaxed, valued, important. My first real long-term exposure to someone different from me. I remember being told to get our rugs for naps and how quiet and still the room would be. Peaceful. There were activities, games and learning done there. I loved to learn. All the students in class looked like me and we all got along.

I liked school.

To this day I remember many, if not most of my elementary school teachers.

First grade was the wonderful Miss (or Mrs. Meadowlark, the quintessential older, graceful, kind and concerned brown-skinned teacher who taught us the beginning steps of reading. I remember sitting in the reading circle reading the Dick and Jane books with Mrs. Meadowlark gently guiding us, helping us to pronounce those tough words, never berating any child at any time (that would come in third grade).

A gentle, light-skinned African American, was my second grade teacher. Another wonderful experience with a dedicated teacher.

However things changed after second grade. I was introduced to stress and pressure and tension, but I didn't know it then. Just knew how I felt. Third grade was traumatic and I no longer liked school. In fact I dreaded going to my third grade home room. You see I met and was taught by Ms. Evil herself. A light-skinned, African American who could have played a witch in anybody's production and would not have been cast against type. If she didn't like you, you knew it.

She played favorites and had certain kids who were her pets. If you were not one of those fortunate few two or three, it could make for a long, fear filled day. She was mean spirited and petty with an irritating voice that was like scratching fingernails on a black chalkboard. The majority of us children in her class seemed beneath her.

These were the days of corporal punishment and by goodness if a student didn't perform as Ms. Evil thought they should, whether it was getting a low score on a quiz or providing a wrong answer to a question in class, the unlucky student was likely to get a swat or two from her ever present paddle. She seemed to relish those moments. She'd make a big production to make sure the pant leg was tight against the leg, which heightened the anxiety, before administering the abusive swat. Boys and girls. Pants or dresses. Didn't make any difference. Sometimes students were called to line up to walk through the coat closet that paralleled our room, a door at each end.

Inside the coat closet was sheer terror. The paddle.

Students fighting, playing or talking, snickering, giggling, or talking under the breath. Of course, those things happened and swats were administered for those who gravely misbehaved. But there wasn't much of that at all in our classroom. We knew better and those who didn't learned quickly.

But the paddle also bit some of us who did not misbehave. We were paddled for any number of other reasons. Or punished for insufficient reasons. Far too often there was definitely a lack of probable or any cause.

For example, if we didn't do well, or what was expected, on some assignment like getting a 70 when Miss Evil thought you should have gotten a 72. Her apparent objective: to beat learning into us.

Learned a lot about life in that classroom. Fear. Intimidation. Unfairness. Hostility. Discrimination (intraracial, class, social). Black on black hatred. It was the children of the so called professional parents that tended to be Miss Evil's pets. Yes, I learned a lot from Miss Evil. Power. Bullying. How to despise authority. We changed classrooms for certain subjects including music, which brings me to other harsh memories with Ms. Evil's partner in crime. Miss Evil's personality twin, a music teacher, Ms. (or Miss?) Sadistic. Although Miss Evil was sadistic, the name fit the dark-skinned, slender, tall, thirty-something instructor to a "t." Same tactics as Miss Evil but Miss Sadistic savored paddling students like a cat creeping upon a cornered mouse. It seemed her eyes glistened with joy every time she could line up students for swats, either on the behind with her paddle, or on the palm of the open hand with her ever present ruler.

"One – two and three – four!" She would tap her ruler on the desktop where she sat like a queen on a throne.

"You missed it," she'd bellow when someone missed a beat on the rhythm scale, "come on up here!"

Slowly striding to the front of the room the next victim would stand next to Miss Sadistic's tidy, well organized wooden desk. We all knew the drill. Hold your hand out, palm up and face her. Bam!

Time after time. You get the picture.

Butterflies not just danced but raged in the stomach. Nerves on edge. Legs shaking.

High anxiety. Don't remember very many if any good times in those two classrooms. I do remember a lot of stress and tension.

Sometimes Miss Sadistic wore this hot pink, polyester dress with matching fur collar. Even a third grader could see how ridiculous she looked. Although decades old the colorful, outrageous memory of this woman dressed to the 9's remains vivid.

I learned that just because some people look like you doesn't mean those people even like you. Or themselves. Yet things did get better, much better, the next year.

Fourth grade with Mrs. Parks restored my faith and hope in teachers who looked like me. Fair, considerate, nice with a sense of humor her classroom was a wonderful respite from third grade. Fifth grade brought contact with another Caucasian homeroom teacher, Miss Hamil. If third grade was the pit experience, Miss Hamil's classroom was the mountaintop. Middle aged with golden blonde hair which seemed to match the color of her car, a 1966 Olds Tornado. Did I love that car!

I learned just how nice a teacher could be. This teacher was not only thoughtful but respectful to us as people. She made us feel important, loved, and Miss Hamil clearly loved being with us. She also made learning challenging but fun. She was a teacher's teacher.

And there were perks to being in her class. On any given day Miss Hamil might hand out peppermint candy to willing takers. Other days we might play games (during recess of course) but Miss Hamil made the games, and everything else, fun. There was time for class work but none of the stress and pressure forked out by some people who looked like us.

During these latter grades from third to sixth students changed class rooms and teachers for certain subjects and some of these teachers were Caucasian. In school there were a few biracial and other minority students but no Caucasian students that I can remember.

Which made the day our class attended a Caucasian elementary school unique and memorable.

I don't know if it was just the sixth grade classes or if there were other grades from Ingalls who participated in the exchange with a Caucasian elementary school; one day our class went to their school and later they attended ours.

When we visited their school we attended some type of assembly. There were several boys on stage playing music in a rock and roll band. I was very impressed. No one at our school played rock music in a band.

After this class exchange our class talked about the experience. It was the first time any of us had been around Caucasian students in a classroom setting. Some liked it and others did not.

Our homeroom teacher asked our opinions of the other students and asked a question during our discussion of race relations:

"How many of you think you could marry a white person?"

Several of us raised our hands.

Her eyes twinkled, a look between amazement and hopeful expectation on her face.

"This might be the generation that does it, that turns things around," she mused aloud.

Little did I know then how interracial relationships would shape the 31 days (nights) of my life.

Day 2
The "N" Word: 1960s (Muskogee, Oklahoma)

"Who's that n***?"

It was perhaps my earliest foray into the suffocating and contradictory jungle of racial self-hate and racist oppression. The question wasn't asked by a Caucasian oppressor but by a descendant of slavery, a product of centuries of human degradation and marginalization.

As a matter of fact it was a question asked by one of my great grandfathers.

His seventy-something old eyes could see clearly who had entered the small, clean, well organized home he shared with his second wife. Traveling to his small town Oklahoma home while in my early teens in junior high school, I entered his home and heard that greeting. Who he was talking about, myself or mother?

Regardless that's how he posed the question.

I wasn't shocked or surprised. That's just how grandpa talked. Period.

Never heard him say colored or Negro (and certainly not black, as that was decades before that moniker was adopted for polite use).

To Grandpa, if a person were black, that person was a n*** and if a person were Caucasian, the person was a peckerwood. Thus this grandfather called everybody who was black, family notwithstanding, the n-word.

Never heard Mother or Pop call anybody the n-word, although for years Pop referred to blacks as "colored." In the mid to late 70's he came around to using the term "black." I certainly heard other relatives use the n-word even after it became politically incorrect and offensive to do so.

I even remember one person, referring to her fellow church members, her church family, not as Christians or brothers or sisters, but "those n***s up there."

The n-word was commonplace in conversation, whether innocent or serious, with family, friends, acquaintances, etc.

Was it a term of endearment as some argue? Was it a word that described a common bond among people? Was it a term that embodied a common feeling, a unifying presence, a shared experience?

Or was it a word filled with poisonous hate, purposefully but covertly administered into the subtle subconscious of a people to disenfranchise, marginalize and incapacitate self-worth and self-esteem for infinite generations?

To be clear, I used the word for years, and didn't see the hurt nor harm. But one day, perhaps due to an epiphany, my attitude changed. I realized just how that six-letter word strips away dignity and integrity and pollutes the intellect, how it, like rancid food, manifests a stench so strong it clouds all judgment.

So I stopped using the n-word. Perhaps it was due to the birth of my children, realizing that someday not only would they hear the word, but, unfortunately, they would be called that hurtful, insulting name. Sooner or later. Directly or indirectly. Expressed or implied.

I never used the word around my children and avoided those people, family and friends included, who did. It just wasn't a word I wanted to take up residence in our home. Didn't want that word to occupy important space in my children's minds, or in my mind.

But it is not going away. Been around too long on people's lips and in their minds, their hearts. Unfortunately.

31 Days (Nights) has other incidents directly involving the n-word. Can't keep people from saying it. It makes and leaves an impression. Don't let it suffocate your spirit or drown your joy. Ever. You are not that word. Never accept or believe it.

Just remember who you are.
What you are.
Precious. Wonderful. Outstanding.
A child of the living God.
Beloved.

Day 3
"Special" Visitors and Sunday Church: 1960s (Wichita, Kansas)

Bright sun rays bouncing off the tan brick walls of a black Baptist church in Wichita, Kansas. The day seemed like any other Sunday morning, the usual, traditional routine. Same folk. Same order of worship service. Same songs. Same preacher. Same deacons. Same same same. Had no reason to expect anything different.

It was a rather pleasant day I do remember, not the cold, harsh winter season, though blustery, hostile Midwestern weather might better mirror the minds and hearts of that predominantly black congregation.

I've never forgotten this Sunday, perhaps because I remember observing from a slight distance. This experience was my initial introduction to let's say, religious insensitivity, maybe even intolerance. You know, the "them and us" or better yet, "them versus us" mentality.

I saw that "we are all not the same" even in the church house. Perhaps "especially" at the church house.

Visiting was middle-aged Caucasian couple who stood outside of the church building, just off the steps, talking to a couple of the church leaders. Not the pastor nor any of the ministers, but deacons.

The couple was dressed appropriately as if they were going to worship, and the man towered over the woman. Did not hear the conversation with our church deacons. Did not see when or if they ever stepped inside the church.

I was glad they were there, I remember thinking. I was a teenager. What did I know about interracial worship? Just thought it was nice they were there.

Apparently that feeling wasn't shared by some others.

In short. Unwelcome. Not here. Go elsewhere.

Was surprised at that sour reaction. This was, after all, a church composed of Christians, believers, in God, in Jesus Christ, in the Holy Spirit where people loved EVERYBODY.

Not really. Not quite. Not EVERYBODY.

What did I really know?

Years later I would come to understand that some folks apparently didn't even LIKE some others in the congregation. There was a lot of back bitin' and back stabbin' in that church.

My church.

It follows if some felt this way about other "brothers and sisters" in their own church, then outsiders wouldn't have a chance. So to think that LOVE would actually spill over onto someone else, someone different, was like believing a camel could go through the eye of a needle.

Back to the visiting couple.

Perhaps they wanted something. Money. Food. Housing.

Maybe it was more. Maybe they were looking for trouble. They stopped by to stir up things, take something away. Maybe they stopped by to oppress and persecute the already disenfranchised and marginalized. Maybe.

Or maybe they were looking for some Good News ... maybe even the Gospel.

Maybe they wanted to hear the Word. Maybe they were in need of a friend. Maybe they needed to see a kind face, a welcoming smile. Maybe they needed to feel some love. Maybe they were even searching for God.

Too bad. It wouldn't be theirs then and there.

"Let them go to their own church." That's how one church member put it. Harsh. Blunt. Cold.

I was shocked at that attitude. Didn't understand it then but years later would come to understand that statement, and more.

Dr. Martin Luther King, Jr. said that 11:00 am on Sunday was still the most segregated hour in America, indicating segregation in worship.

But New Testament scripture advises that we should be careful how we treat people, specifically strangers, for at times unknown to us we have entertained angels. Lot of theology in that scripture.

Wonder what ever happened to that couple, where they went, what they did. Not only that day, but what happened in their lives. They are probably dead but the memory and their image lingers on in my mind.

That particular church building is long gone, demolished and the membership moved to another, larger, nicer area with a new, modern sanctuary added to an existing building.

I wonder if many of the minds and hearts have changed. Of course, the old guard is gone, dead, but in some situations old attitudes and views are just replaced with new people carrying the same attitudes and views.

Yes, learned a very valuable lesson that summer, spring, or fall Sunday morning.

The seasons change but sometimes the hard, biting cold of winter lasts much, much longer in some hearts than a few months of the year.

Day 4
Aunt's Voice: 1960s (Wichita, Kansas)

A relative worked as a receptionist/secretary/administrative assistant for a small business in the 1960s. She was "professional" to the "t" in all senses of the word. Knew her stuff and then some. Knew how to carry herself, a black woman in corporate America. This was in the shadow of the Civil Rights Movement, after the 1963 March on Washington, after the deaths of Medgar, Malcolm and Martin, after the passing of the Civil Rights and Voting Rights laws.

Often my Aunt So-and-So would stop by our house after work with a box of delicious, glazed donuts. Immaculate and well-coiffed, she knew how to dress and act the part. Intelligent with a quick wit, this depression era woman fit in and was an integral part of her business family.

Regardless of the circumstance or situation, she was flawless in her transformation. Including her voice.

This aunt often called my mother, her sister, on the phone, and when I was old enough to notice, I noticed the change in her voice, in her speaking when she talked to "us," meaning family, friends, church folk. She talked and sounded like us. Don't get me wrong, she still had consistent and proper subject–verb agreement and never spoke in broken English. Yet she "sounded" like us.

Until she talked on the telephone. The phone itself was the instrument of change.

Say what?

I started to notice how she sounded in conversation when talking to someone who was not one of "us," especially in a business context. Specifically how my aunt talked to Caucasian people.

Aunt So-and-So sounded different. Vastly different. Her articulation, pronunciation, tone, inflection, enunciation, diction, delivery, all changed. She was still Aunt So-and-So, but she was also different. If I didn't know it was Aunt So-and-So I would have believed this was a different person from a different race.

In short, the voice on the phone did not belong to a black person.

Not to say she was attempting to sound Caucasian, but she certainly didn't sound "black." When I was younger I noticed but didn't understand. When I got older, teenager, even as a young adult, I realized she was consciously speaking differently and I still didn't understand.

Wondered why and began to think it was unnecessary. Putting up a false front. Projecting an image of a false reality.

At first, I admit, when the realization struck as to what she was doing and why, I was both embarrassed and ashamed. For the role I thought she had to play.

"Be yourself" I naively concluded.

Then, in time, I started to understand.

Aunt was not forced to play any role. She chose to disguise herself to manipulate/confuse the enemy rooted, wrapped and designed to disenfranchise and marginalize all those who it tags as "other" and "less than."

Much later when teaching college level communications course, I ran across the concept of "identity management," defined by scholars Ronald B. Adler, G. Rodman and A. du Pre in a textbook titled *Understanding Human Communication* as "Strategies used by communicators to influence the way others view them." They call it "face switching," explained as "Adopting the perspectives of different cultures."

BINGO!

Aunt understood that in playing the game of life when the deck is already stacked against certain folks and systemic racism is deeply ingrained throughout all levels and segments of society, there are no "rules," no "limits," no "boundaries and no "standards" to prejudice, discrimination, inequality, and disparate treatment.

Aunt knew and understood the game and played it well. A country girl from a large, poor family who learned how to beat the oppressive, privileged, arrogant, racist system by playing the game on her terms.

Yes, Aunt learned through her voice, there were some things she could control.

Out of sight.

Aunt outfoxed the fox.

Day 5
Names: Sticks and Stones: 1969-71 (Wichita, Kansas)

"Sticks and stones can break my bones but names will never hurt me!"
A sing-songy ditty I heard as a child.
Unfortunately, one of society's biggest lies.
Names, words, do hurt. For years. Can rip apart self-esteem. Can slice more effectively than a sharpened Thanksgiving Day turkey carving knife. Can weigh heavier in the mind than a two-ton boulder. Can outlive and contaminate longer than the nastiest cockroach.
Word power. Some may argue the only power is what the victim allows (like victims "allow" abuse). But it is not a matter of "allowing." Minds are, conscious or subconscious, rather complex yet automatic recorders. The words are there. They remain. Period.
I've been called names. Some good, some not so good. Some complimentary, encouraging and some degrading, disheartening. And some downright cruel and mean.
Like the stink of morning breath. You get the picture.
And names can make lasting impressions. Not just on you. On others.
Example: In elementary school, fifth or sixth grade, I used to wear a myriad of hats and caps to school. Took pride in my collection of brims. A creative way of expression.
Was home standing out in the backyard (maybe doing some light yard work with mother) and another student, a guy in a grade higher, strolled by. He looked into our yard and saw me.
"Hey Mr. Cool!" he shouted. At me.
"Hey" or something along those lines I answered.
Mother was not only surprised and amused, but as I could tell in her voice as she told the story to an aunt, a bit impressed.
I've never forgotten that.
Contrast that with another experience with three black "sisters" from my "hood."

They were neighbors who lived right around the corner or down the street. That close.

They could actually smell the same polluted, oppressed air.

We were students at the recently integrated Mayberry Junior High School, bused there to achieve integration. Two of the "sisters" were 7th graders, as I was. The third an eighth grader. They always hung together. Three peas in a pod. Eeny - Meany - and Miney. I guess they missed Moe.

Actually, they were more like three blind mice.

One bright, sunny day when school was over, I stepped onto our rapidly filling bus, the old, weather-beaten and ragged vehicle that took us from our homes in the "hood" in northeast Wichita to the west side school several miles across town. I sat down toward the middle of the bus next to a kid, "Red" Darnell. I couldn't help but notice the cacophony of sounds coming from the rear of the bus.

"Here comes Tom! Here comes Tom!"

A nasty chorus from the three before mentioned Supremes which I chose to, at first, ignore. But couldn't help but hear their poison filled words.

Didn't know who the poor target was of those bombarding inflammatory bombs of disrespect and humiliation.

Then Red, with his fair complexion, freckles and burning red hair brought it all home.

"You hear what they are saying about you?"

"They aren't talking about me!" was my naïve response.

But they were. I wanted to dive in between the ugly, worn, brown seats, trying but failing to cover my head in the sand of junior high pride. I tried to ignore the sting of ignorance, the bitter blow of stupidity but could not.

Was I seated in the window seat or was the aisle, I can't remember. Regardless, kept a steely hardened gaze on the outside, focused on the busy activity, the apparent freedom beckoning in the parking lot. My body was trapped in an intolerable, hostile situation while my mind sought escape.

"Why?" I wondered afterwards.

I had not said or done anything to any of them at any time. Ever. Even thought, foolishly, they were among my "friends." But this revisited a succinct, brick hard lesson about life delivered in the language of the streets:

"Sometimes your friends ain't your friends."

Oh I don't remember how long it went on, whether it stopped shortly thereafter or continued for several minutes. Regardless it was bullying 1970s style.

It happened and I remember. Even after all these years. Most importantly I remember how I felt.

And I thought, this was my fault!

What can I do to make things better?

That evening after the incident I actually made phone calls to two of the perpetrators.

Wanted to know what I was doing, what I needed to change.

I was really trying to get along, willing to do anything to fit into and belong in their world. To be acceptable, if not accepted.

Dialed Kim's phone number, one of the 7th graders, but couldn't reach her.

Reached Renee, the 8th grader. She said that I needed to act more, be more "black."

I didn't quite know what that meant.

I had no more Caucasian "acquaintances" than any of the other "brothers." Maybe even fewer.

She couldn't really articulate what acting "black" was. And I really didn't know what that meant. I remember saying that I would do that, whatever that was, that would make me "blacker" and catapult me back into the three Sisters' good graces.

I had no more problems with those three after that and for a while I was, whatever that meant, thinking "black." Not cussing, not talking smack or loud, not smoking weed, not trashing girls, not acting like I didn't have brain or sense God gave a goose, but trying my best to act like a brother. In reality, I didn't act much different than before.

Then the light bulb turned on. I realized I was, at least in my mind, trying to conform, to please someone else and not be who I was. Me, myself and I.

Being a "brother" was who I was by nature of birth. There is no set definition of a brother or description of what or how a brother is supposed to act, with the exception of being true to yourself, mind, spirit and soul within the context of your family, cultural, racial, ethnic, or social heritage.

Complex and complicated, yet in some ways, not.

It's a matter of recognizing, acknowledging and respecting one's roots.

I tried being a "brother" for the previously mentioned trio for a while until I got tired of wearing that ill fitted mask. The credit goes to football great Jim Brown.

Yes, that Jim Brown, the great Hall of Fame running back for the Cleveland Browns.

A major magazine, i.e., *Life* or *Look*, published a feature profile story on Brown complete with color photos.

They say, "Knowledge is power" and that article certainly played an influential role in my life.

Jim Brown told his critics, those who didn't see or seek to understand who he was, that he could care less. Well, that's not quite how he put it.

Actually, it was more like "I'm me and I don't give a d----."

It was his life, his thoughts, his attitude. Other people cannot and would not be allowed to run his life. His words empowered me.

I could be Me, whoever Me was!

Jim Brown made so much sense and at that critical time in my life it was exactly what I needed. Those words, on pages of a widely circulated magazine, spoke truth to power for me.

I am me and I don't give a d___!

My attitude began to change. And it showed. I became more determined, more focused, more *ME*. And people like the three amigos didn't matter. Anybody else whom I deemed negative could say or do what they chose.

Couldn't control them, their attitudes or their behavior.

But my reaction would be the same.

Frankly I don't give a _____.

The Sistas from the hood knew it, saw it and felt it.

In short, they ceased to exist in my world. They became In–vis–ible.

Fast forward several months.

I began to come into my own, who I wanted to be. I finished junior high, on my terms.

The transformation continued in high school. Growing into myself.

That traumatic 7th grade incident helped shape who I would become.

I hardly saw any of my former tormentors during the high school years.

I liked who I became: eyes and mind opened, head held up, I walked tall.

Post Script. Decades have passed. Never saw any of the three girls after those teen years. But when I think of them, I remember that day, long ago.

Bullying, judgment, condemnation, and ridicule.

Yet the pain produced power, grit and determination.

And I rose. Transformed.

Resurrected!

Day 6
Mrs. Reed/Mayberry Hall Monitor:1969-72 (Wichita, Kansas)

Willowy, slight build, short stature with snow white hair and wire rimmed glasses, hands with a grip strong as iron, this tough as nails educator sternly patrolled the Mayberry Junior High halls. I knew of her well before I enrolled in her Algebra class. Her reputation far exceeded her.

Every student knew who she was and few dared to either misbehave, act up or cross her in that junior high jungle.

Mrs. Lily Reed was respected if not feared.

This was well before the age of defiance and disobedience, well before children took over schools and intimidated teachers. Well before the now common occurrence of student on student, student on teacher deadly violence manifested in a plethora of ways. Echoes of the last days of innocence in schools when students still respected adults for being adults.

Mrs. Reed maintained order, structure, discipline, respect, a code of proper conduct. If not, this little lady would snatch your arm and off to the office for a visit with the principal.

She was the Mayberry hall traffic cop.

It was 1969 and the first year of busing for integration but Mrs. Reed didn't discriminate.

Actually, it was the Caucasian kids who usually drew her wrath. I don't remember many of us black students earning her unwanted attention. If so, it was rare and deserved.

Didn't know Mrs. Reed when I first saw her in action. Because of her reputation, I thought she was the meanest person in the school. I wasn't alone either.

Many black students had her pegged, bones made of callous prejudice with cloudy eyes of bias and favoritism.

Little did we know. Many teens and junior high youngsters were full of assumptions and attitudes and short of common sense and experience. And don't even mention the word "wisdom."

When I finally enrolled in Mrs. Reed's Algebra class as a 9th grader, I found a teacher who was efficient, organized and, most importantly, patient, understanding, considerate, even kind.

Don't get me wrong, she kept firm control of her class and students: there was discipline and structure.

The bottom line: Mrs. Reed cared, I would discover later.

During the spring there was always a 9th grade dance and Mrs. Reed was there. My mother was one of the parents who chaperoned the event. Mother not only met Mrs. Reed but, shocking me, engaged in conversation with her. Very enlightening conversation.

In class I'd noticed that Mrs. Reed seemed to have a special relationship with a sweet natured Native American girl. Not that she treated her as a favorite but clearly there was something about the girl that attracted her attention.

I found out why. Mother learned, to my amazement, that Mrs. Reed, the hateful, bigoted, evil hall monitor, was married to a Native American. I never would have guessed it.

So much for all those accusations of her being prejudiced and biased against blacks and other oppressed people. Mrs. Reed knew, had lived with discrimination and oppression up close and very personal.

Well what do you know?!

My perception of Mrs. Reed was never the same.

Finished Mayberry and on to high school. Then to college. Then to grad school. Then...the real world, jobs, the rat race, etc.

I was working as a news reporter in Des Moines, Iowa in the early 1980s when Mother got a phone call from, yep, that's right, Mrs. Reed!

After all those years! Mrs. Reed just wanted to check and see how I was doing. And an unlikely, unexpected friendship began.

She offered her help if I needed any with math in grad school courses. I didn't but we stayed in contact. When I returned to town I made a point to visit Mrs. Reed and had the opportunity to meet her husband.

Wonderful woman! Wonderful family! I was truly blessed!

When I married, her name was on the guest list. She couldn't make it but, get this: This seventy-something lady caught several buses from her south Wichita home, to leave a wedding gift at my home in the "hood" in northeast Wichita! Her present: a *Leaves of Gold* book of wisdom readings which still sits proudly in a bookcase.

I visited with Mrs. Reed many times over the years and learned lots of things from her ranging from the serious--the prejudice she experienced as the spouse of a Native American--to the unique and unexpected--despite her senior years she owned a Corvette sports car!

We kept in touch for several years until her health failed and she moved out of her longtime home.

Mrs. Reed was much more than what she appeared to be. Looks can certainly be deceiving. I was reminded to never judge a book by its cover.

Open the book on Mrs. Reed and the chapters reveal an amazing, inspiring woman.

I can still hear her voice today giving encouragement and hope. "Yes you can do it" and "you hang on."

Mrs. Reed was far more than a junior high hall monitor and math teacher.

This stellar teacher's teacher was indeed a blessing.

Lily Margaret Stevens Reed.

Gift from God.

Day 7
Victory: Mr. Student Council President: 1971-72 (Wichita, Kansas)

"Power to the People!"
That's how I started my speech to the Mayberry Junior High student body during the assembly to decide student council officers for my 9th grade year. I don't know how, or why I got the idea to run but I thought I could do just as well as anyone else.

Keep in mind this was a predominantly Caucasian school, located on the west side of town and this was the second year of the Wichita school desegregation program (i.e., busing black students from the northeast section of Wichita to predominantly white schools elsewhere in the city).

To my knowledge no other black student had ever attempted to run for office at Mayberry.

So. First time for everything.

We ran as teams, presidential and vice presidential candidates. My teammate was a wonderful friend I'd known for many years and we had shared several elementary school classes: Vaniece. Her birthday was the day before mine and many years I enjoyed going to her birthday parties.

As I remember, there were two or three other "teams" running for the position. All other teams were Caucasian students.

But I was not to be discouraged. This was part of the "new" me, doing my own thing my own way regardless of what anyone else thought.

And I thought that not only could we win, but we could do a good job as representatives of and for the students.

It was not lost on me the color issue, but we had support of a cross section of students: African American, Caucasian, northeast side, extreme west side (even then I understood the importance of demographics).

I understood that I had to both grab and hold the attention and interest of the student body with my speech. It could not be boring, status quo and lackluster.

It had to be different. It had to be powerful. It had to be creative.

It had to strike a chord with and appeal to a cross section of the student body.

And it also had to illustrate that not only could I do the job, but I could do it better than the other candidates.

So what to do and how to do it?

At the time there was a song with the lyrics, "Power to the people, you got to give the people what they want" by an African American soul/funk/rhythm and blues band. And that's where I got the idea to lead with that opening statement for my speech.

"Power to the people!"

Unlike the other presidential candidates I was not dressed in a coat and tie but in a "mod" 1960s hippie style V-neck silk shirt with a matching belt that I wore outside of/over my slacks. I purposely chose that shirt to look "hip" or "cool" and anti-establishment.

And my mother, an excellent seamstress, made that shirt.

I don't remember the order in which we spoke nor if our vice presidential teammates made any comments.

I do remember when it was my turn I stepped to the microphone, looked across the auditorium's sea of faces, and with confidence spoke the first words out of my mouth, the forceful, assertive statement:

"Power to the people!"

I remember and actually was surprised at the raucous, excited reaction from the crowd!

To this day I believe those first three words won the election for us.

In retrospect, I remember the student council meetings where I presided as president.

I remember some of the other activities and assemblies in which I participated.

I remember the support and encouragement from many other students as well as faculty and staff.

I remember two essential lessons learned at that early age: to achieve one must first believe and dreams can come true.

And regardless of what some may think or say, set the goal, try, and know that people of all walks of life will hear and accept your message.

People will believe in you if you believe in them. And yourself. Be real, true to yourself.

Day 8
West High School Senior/Football: 1974-75 (Wichita, Kansas)

Why didn't I get to play? I was mystified. Just didn't understand it.

Was it me? Questions in my mind regarding my football career as a senior at Wichita West High School.

Backdrop to the story. I generally started on Coach (later Dr.) Jerry Goodman's sophomore football team my first year of playing organized football. The wishbone was our offensive formation. It featured the quarterback and three running backs: a fullback and two halfbacks, positioned behind the fullback. I played halfback.

I was the fastest on the squad, but the bottom line is I don't remember ever being tackled for a loss in the backfield during a game. Despite this experience, I never got called up to play varsity, and neither did any other sophomore.

Junior year was vastly different. Bright, hot and steamy August two-a-day practices with the varsity squad were tough. Stayed out as long as I could but eventually I quit before school started and two-a-day football practices--mornings and late afternoons—ended.

Knew that things would have been easier if I could have lasted but despite my best efforts, just couldn't hang in there long enough.

To be frank, I just couldn't take it, the bruises, the sore muscles, the aching joints. As Mother put it, I was constantly "stoved up." Varsity was still running the wishbone but football, despite my hopes and dreams of staying on the team, just wasn't working out for me. Looking back on it that decision to leave the team just might have had a ripple effect on what did, or did not, happen for me during my senior year.

My senior year was my final chance. I'd try it again, determined to not just make it through two-a-day practices and stay on the team but to play. Did everything I thought the head football coach asked even before school started.

It started with the summer informal "get togethers" (my words).

Athletes would go out to West High or other places (even a lake) to "be together." Did not work on plays or formations but we did various forms of conditioning exercises such as weight lifting and running.

Did that and everything else. Most of all remember pinning my hopes on thinking I had a "fair" minded coach, one who would at least give me a chance. And I listened closely to every word he uttered.

Remember once during one of these "get togethers" someone asked coach who would play quarterback. He hemmed and hawed claiming he didn't know and mentioned several names. Then added one that caught me completely off guard: mine.

"Reggie" or perhaps it was "Reg-o", coach had a teasing way of manipulating names.

When I heard that I was shocked. Never played at that position before but it gave me hope.

I thought, "Hey, if I'm not at quarterback, which I've never played, surely I will play at one of the halfback spots where I do have experience." Surely.

Little did I know.

Got past those rough two-a-days: the Oklahoma drill, the chicken fights, the "rah rah, let's go WEST!" chants. But imagine my surprise when the season started and I was not listed among the starters. Was more than mildly surprised, shocked was more like it.

"What's the deal?"

And it was just the first week. Then the second, the third and so on. I kept waiting, trying to keep my spirits up. Trying not to show my keen disappointment, actually, my embarrassment.

Why? How's that?

At the practices I thought, foolishly, "put out your best at practice, show what you can do, you will get in. He will have to put you in." And it was what happened at practice that kept me encouraged.

I would often practice at halfback with the first team or alternate. That's good, or so I thought. And I had some wonderful, exciting practices. In short, after a while, I made the practices my game experience.

One time, mid to late season, with the first or second team offense going against first team defense, head coach called a sweep and wanted the defense to stop it.

After receiving the ball from the center, the quarterback quickly pitched the ball to one of the halfbacks who ran wide or "sweeps" around the eighth hole, i.e., around the end.

Everybody heard the play called. I was the ball carrier and the target with the bull's eye in the center of my shoulder pads.

I line up knowing that 11 players will be coming after me.

"Let them come, catch me if you can…"

The ball was snapped as the quarterback effortlessly pitched the pigskin to me.

Whoosh! I took the ball around the end, turned the corner up field and swept all right, swept untouched to the end zone! Through coach's precious first team defense.

"Take that!" I thought.

Head coach is not pleased with his defense. What does he do? He calls the exact same play again. Everybody knows who is coming. Me. Same offense, same defense, same play, same runner, same everything. I took it personal. He was setting me up. That's all right. But I am insulted!

Quarterback goes to the line, ball is hiked, and again the pitch is perfect and …whoosh!

I sweep around the same end, rush through the same defense for the very same result. Untouched. All the way to the end zone! Again! An exact replay!

I remember one defensive player congratulating me.

"I just want to play! Let me try this in an actual game, let me try!"

But not on his team. Absolutely nothing changed.

I never played in any varsity game.

Regardless of how badly the game was out of hand, how few minutes were left on the clock, how badly we were losing. Our team only won one game, the first, against Ark City, 21-6.

Lost the other eight. Some were close, others rather lopsided. I played only on junior varsity.

But if Coach wanted a "spokesman" I was good enough for that, whether being asked to make comments to the team after a particularly devastating loss or as one of several football student athlete symbols for the school.

Was I a token? Good enough for symbolism, but not to play.

Despite my hopes and dreams I did not earn a West High School varsity football letter for my senior year. Despite all the time, work, sweat, and pain. Apparently did not make any difference to the coaches.

Prior to all of this I'd heard from other black players that the head coach was prejudiced. He wasn't even Caucasian and certainly didn't look white. Some said he had Native American blood. Whatever. Coach apparently had bits of racism and pieces of bigotry in his bloodline as well.

I just didn't want to believe it, wanted to give him the benefit of the doubt.

Often tried to rationalize and justify. Maybe he was watching out for me, didn't want to risk my subsequent track season with an injury. Maybe this ... maybe that. Regardless, he didn't let me play.

One thing about life, it will provide the same lesson over and over until that lesson is learned. Although it took a while to gather all the pieces, I did finish that puzzle.

A significant puzzle piece (and lingering question): Was it due to my girlfriend Margaret being Caucasian?

Was it my innovative football cleats. White but with a circular, rotating disc that the cleats were attached to. They were rare, unusual, and I remember one assistant football coach questioning me about those shoes. No other player on the team had those.

Was it because I simply didn't fit his notion of what a black teenager should look like? Should act like? Had my own relatively new car. Had clothes on my back (thanks to Pop and Mother). Made good grades.

Or was it because I left his team my junior year?

Was it this? Was it that? (Fill in the blank).

Maybe I wasn't "good enough" to start but not even to play? On a losing team at that? My thought was if I was good enough to play for Dr. Goodman a few years earlier, I should have been good enough to play on a varsity team with many of the same players.

I figured it out later, fitting together my own experience with the experiences and comments of others. Others who should know.

The man was indeed prejudiced, biased and a bigot, all wrapped in one.

Unfortunately. For many of us.

I never tried organized football again. Perhaps I should have.

Perhaps I should have tried again at the small college I enrolled in just out of high school, Baker University.

But I didn't. Just didn't care. Burned once by a football coach why should I be vulnerable again.

Yet, I do remember some good times with good friends who helped pull me through that senior year of football. And I can say "I was a football player!"

"Slot right 26 power on two, hut!"

Day 9
Racial Profiling – DWB – First Time: 1974-75 (Wichita, Kansas)

Life is filled with "firsts."
First time going to school.
First time riding a bike.
First love.
Those "firsts" tend to be memorable, impressionable and often positive.
But not always.
Some of those firsts are negative, painful and life changing if not life threatening.
And with some of us, the firsts include, unfortunately some ugly racial incidents.
First time feeling the sting of being treated differently.
First time being left out or left behind.
First time feeling "less than."
First time being treated as invisible.
Or, alternatively, being afforded "special" treatment. Drawing unmerited, undeserved attention.
Being profiled. Being shadowed, i.e., followed while either retail shopping or just looking.
Being met with discriminatory, steely, cold, hostile glares.

The first times with the police too often become dangerous times and, tragically, last times.
Remember the first time I was stopped driving while black by the police.
I was 17 years old and was cruising, alone, in my shiny 1973 two tone gold-trimmed-in-white Ford Maverick Grabber. The car had a very distinctive color scheme. Driving in my neighborhood I was only four to five blocks away from home passing in front of my old elementary school. The car was properly licensed and I was breaking

no traffic laws. Glancing in my rear view mirror, I saw the police cruiser behind me.

There was no high speed chase, nor any attempt to elude or escape. What for? Wasn't doing anything, just minding my own business. Didn't matter.

Suddenly with a flip of a switch came that blasting siren and flashing red lights disturbing the peace of a sunny, pleasant afternoon.

"What is this?" I mused to myself. Wasn't afraid or even uncomfortable as I had done absolutely nothing.

I stopped and the young officer approached my car. I am sure he asked for my license and registration, but I don't remember that. What I remember about the conversation is that I asked why I was stopped.

"A car matching this description was used in a robbery..." was the officer's response.

And that's when I realized why I was stopped: I was young, black and driving a nice car.

But there was something else I realized up close and personal. Police lie.

As mentioned, my car had a very distinctive paint job and only a fool or someone with less than common sense would use that type of vehicle in the commission of any kind of crime. But the officer expected me to believe his fabrication. I didn't then and never have.

But in my naivety I asked a question that showed just how little I knew about the dangerous threat of being in police custody.

I asked if we needed to go downtown. "No, we don't have to do that."

No, I wasn't afraid, and it was clear I was not in violation of any law. I was willing to go downtown and get this matter resolved. I knew he had no legal basis, no reason, no...

And yes, I was well read and well informed, so I was aware of police violence, brutality and murder. But I also felt that it could not happen then in broad daylight. Not here in the mid-1970s in Wichita, Kansas. And it could not happen to me. Obviously wrong on all fronts; it had happened in Wichita and many other places many times.

Black people hurt and killed at the hands of the police for no reason.

Thanks to God's grace this stop on this day didn't go tragic. The officer returned to his cruiser and I returned to my cruising. But I was different, I had changed. In that short encounter I'd experienced another "first."

Unfortunately.

Day 10
AU & the "N" Word: 1977-78 (Washington, D.C.)

    Was a bright, sunny afternoon and was feeling pretty good walking across the parking lot of Anderson Hall, my dorm at the American University, in Washington, D.C. I'd transferred there officially from Baker University, by way of University of Tulsa, Tulsa, Oklahoma (which I attended in a special one semester mass communications program in the spring, 1977).
    Don't know where I was coming from. Don't know if I had parked my car, the two tone gold and white 1973 Ford Maverick Grabber, the shiny new car that I'd received a whole two months before my 16th birthday.
    Don't know if I was coming from a jog from the athletic stadium. Don't remember. Regardless was minding my own business when floating through the air the word suddenly struck like striking a toe against a chair leg.
    "N***."
    Looked up at the multistory glass and steel structure, seeking the window that caged the offender's cowardly face.
    Can't remember if the voice screamed that venom once or twice.
    My anger rose like the hair on the back of my neck.
    Wanted to see... wanted to find that offender.
    No such luck.
    Where is he? Hiding of course...
    Hiding behind plates of glass, hiding behind a mountain of cement and steel, hiding behind a facade of gentility and politeness, hiding behind the mask of racism and prejudice, but wearing the cloak of ignorance, dressed in privilege and entitlement.
    Thought how foolish this instigator was, to spout an offensive word in this place, Chocolate City, U.S.A., on the hallowed grounds of higher education.
    Showed just how much sense he had.

Showed his level of maturity and security.

But also exposed his weakness.

Easy to do … shout poison from above, on high, anonymously.

Where he couldn't be found. Couldn't be seen. But definitely heard.

First and only time anything like that ever happened to me on a college campus. Ever.

As a student or teacher. But still I remember.

Even now taking my first steps into the lobby of a dorm … I remember.

Searching. Looking. Eyes wide open, primed.

Nothing. Nobody.

Everything the same. Everyone behaving as usual. Nothing or nobody different.

But not me. Ever again.

Optimism clouded. Idealism shaken. Hostility kindled.

Reminded of what's real.

Stupidity. Ignorance. Hatred. Bigotry. Prejudice. Discrimination. Another very real, painful lesson in the pages of life. The ivory towers tarnished and stained.

Day 11
Two Women & AU: 1977-78 (Washington, D.C.)

While a student at American University, a private university located in the Northwest of Washington, D.C., I encountered a lot of folk from across the nation, folk from cultures from different parts of the world. What attracted me to the school was its location in a predominantly black urban environment, especially coming from the Midwest where in almost every instance "we" were not just a minority, we were *the* minority.

D.C., called in some circles "Chocolate City" because of its majority black population, was quite a change for me. Seeing African Americans and other dark-skinned people on campus was no big deal and it was also common to see "us" in various professional capacities and settings.

This was, truly a l-o-n-g way from Kansas, especially Wichita; not only geographically but politically, socially, philosophically, and culturally. Although I was only on campus two semesters (fall 1977 and spring 1978 it didn't take long to experience the wide, rich, deep essence of the black experience. Both the good and the not so good.

My encounters with two similar but yet distinctly different middle-aged black women illustrate my point.

Thin build, caramel color, "Annie" was a pleasant and hard working housekeeper always dressed in her uniform "whites." Usually quiet and reserved, she would come do her work in our dorm and make small talk in response when someone else started the conversation.

Annie was a true professional and much more than the domestic cover in which she was draped.

One very brief snapshot of her life revealed a longing I've always remembered. I overheard Annie tell another student that she'd like to someday travel to Chicago.

"But I don't know if I'll ever make it."

I remember thinking that although Chicago was in the Midwest it really wasn't that far. I really couldn't relate to why a relatively short distance would seem a nearly impossible trek for her.

"Just buy a ticket and go" I naively thought. "No big deal to go to Chicago."

I didn't understand it then but certainly do now after knowing many people like Annie. Time and life bring changes in perspective. Yes, it was a big deal.

It wasn't just the distance but also perhaps it was the other things that trap people into unchanging, immovable, seemingly insurmountable situations. Situations that seem like quicksand in life. Stuck and instead of being able to pull yourself out, sinking deeper and deeper until ...

Maybe there were several agonizing traps that sucked the promise and potential out of Annie's life.

Perhaps cost was one. Maybe she was living paycheck to paycheck stretched to the limit just to survive day-to-day. Any out-of-town trip could be nearly impossible for one scraping to get by to pay the rent/mortgage, food, electricity, gas, phone, multiple insurance premiums, and an array of other of life's cash requirements.

Or it could have been a lingering health condition, either hers or a loved one's, that kept her tied to her home base.

There could have been many other factors as well but I do remember feeling that this pleasant, sweet soul deserved much more in life.

Too bad I couldn't say the same about my other example, Ms. Chocolate Sourpuss. This high falutin' lady worked as a teller at a nearby bank. Always fashionably tailored and finely manicured, she sat on her stool like a queen holding court from a lofty golden throne, with banking customers and students as her lowly, unworthy subjects.

Yes she was that sadity. And mean. Wearing her glasses just off the tip of her nose her penetrating steely glare was as sharp and crisp as a laser beam. There was no compassion in her spirit, no kindness in her halting, pedantic speech. She acted like a prima donna and the bank was her stage. She acted as if she owned the air that we breathed in that place. She was so crabby that I often would try to avoid her line. Just didn't want to deal with her nasty, crusty, snotty, snooty attitude.

She was so sour she could make New Orleans sweet tea bitter.

Of course, I don't know her story. Perhaps she had a reason for being mad at the world. Maybe her personal life was in some type of turmoil causing her to release her frustration on others. Maybe her high heeled, sharp, pointy toed shoes were just too tight and continuously gave her little toe an agonizing pinch, an unrelenting ache.

Whatever pain Ms. Moneybags was in she certainly was successful in transmitting that pain to others, if only in a brief, two minute banking transaction.

A tale of two women, both black and middle aged. Both working in the D.C. area. But a sharp contrast in attitudes and personalities. As different as day and night but both leaving lasting impressions. Yes even after all these years.

What impressions are you leaving? Impressions do matter.

Day 12
Broadcasting/KAKE: 1978 (Wichita, Kansas)

I was on my way!
Was dressed to the nines for my job interview at KAKE -TV, then the top-rated Wichita, Kansas, television station. Made sure I was ready from head to toe for my meeting, everything in place, shirt neatly pressed, tie snug around my neck, shoes polished -- I'd spent years preparing for this moment!

I had graduated from the American University in May, 1978. A very kind campus job/career counselor, knowing I planned to return to Kansas, knew someone at KAKE-TV I could contact, and I certainly followed through. Now this was my shot in the summer of 1978.

This was working out very nicely I thought. Although I had focused my efforts on television journalism, what was available at the time, I was told, was a part time reporting job in the radio department. Fine, if I could get my size 11 ½ foot in the door, who knew where this could lead. Have to start some place, why not there?

Was confident and expectant. I'd been chasing this dream for what 2 ½, 3 years?

It started as an innocent conversation with some friends in a dorm room lounge while watching the news on a Kansas City television station. I'd made the comment, after seeing a black male news reporter, "I'd like to do that." Another freshman, Darryl, a brother from St. Louis, commented, "They won't let you do that!"

I countered with something along the lines that "sure I can" and there it began.

In the meantime I shifted my focus from print journalism to the visual mediums, both television and film and prepared the best way I knew how. After participating in a special Mass Communications program at the University of Tulsa, I'd transferred to the American University where I took film and television classes, completed an internship, and got to know people in the business. I'd left no stone unturned.

But no teacher I had had conversations with in any of my classes, no professionals, including black media personalities, warned me about the gigantic hurdle I would face, the color based obstacle known as ...

Racism.

Of course I was well aware of prejudice and discrimination and had been victimized more than once. But naively I thought, in the real world of broadcasting at this time, things had to be different. Stations were, I heard time after time, looking for qualified minority journalists.

Back to KAKE-TV.

First I met with a couple of programming/news officials. Then, I recorded a demo reading. Then a meeting with Mr. Big, the general manager, president and the community "face" of the station.

After exchanging pleasantries with Mr. Hotshot, "You didn't do very well on your tape," he started.

Caught me off guard. I knew that while it certainly wasn't my best work, it certainly wasn't my worst.

He continued, on a roll.

Mr. Broadcasting claimed I didn't pronounce my words properly, my enunciation needed improvement, my diction was faulty. He proceeded in no uncertain words, to say, in short, that I didn't talk well enough to work at his station.

"We can't use you."

Shocked, surprised, knocked off guard, you name it.

Then he exposed his true colors and what this was really about. Mr. KAKE said I needed to sound like black broadcasters in other places such as Kansas City. "Are you listening, I'm trying to help you," was his clarion call.

What is this? Blatantly comparing me, a kid right out of college with seasoned professionals. Seasoned black professionals that is. I'd taken speech and broadcast announcing courses from the very best of university instructors and never had I been told the things this middle-aged white man was claiming.

Did he require his new Caucasian reporters to sound like broadcast standard bearers at the time such as Walter Cronkite, Peter Jennings, David Brinkley?

I was devastated. Nothing positive, nothing encouraging, nothing hopeful left that man's lips. My heart was shot with the arrows of disappointment, despair, frustration. It is one thing to be rejected; it is quite another to be humiliated, attacked with the intent to destroy opportunities.

This is not at all what I expected, what I hoped I'd find in my return to Wichita. I had worked for nearly three years to prepare myself for a broadcast journalism career and had earned my degree from American University.

I should have known better. Wichita -- a Midwestern city with a Southern attitude when it comes to race.

Racism. Sure I was very much prepared for it in some ways, but in others, I was not. I was being enlightened about the real world of broadcasting; this is how things really worked outside of the ivory covered walls of academia, how it worked in the Air Capital of the World (the home of Beech, Boeing, Cessna and Lear Jet aircraft companies), Wichita, Kansas.

If I'd known this I would have stayed where I was in Washington, D.C., where I saw black people who made their living, some quite successfully, in television journalism.

I thought I could at least get a start in my hometown. KAKE-TV did have, from time to time, a black journalist on television, generally a woman (although for a brief period a local former college basketball player did the sports). At some point I learned that black women were considered "two-fers" (two for one), satisfying both the racial and gender categories for minority hiring statistics.

Of course I knew about the "informal" or "hidden/silent" minority quota and the old excuse that there are no black folk on television because management could never supposedly find any acceptable qualified applicants. Just didn't really believe that was the case in my home town of Wichita, even though I knew there were serious racial issues throughout the community.

I don't remember the other two network affiliates, KARD (NBC) or KTVH (CBS), ever having any black folk employed on camera during this time. I thought my best shot would be the longtime ratings leader and ABC affiliate KAKE-TV.

I had my head in the sand. When I lifted my head, I nearly got it chopped off. Never forgot that incident but, most importantly, never forgot how I felt. All those feelings cited previously, but especially the feeling of being slapped with a lie and expected to accept it as truth. You know The Lie's three parts: "You are not equal, you are not worthy, you are not good enough!"

That's not what I believed then and many decades later I still don't believe it.

Not saying I was perfect, far from it, but I was "good enough" to work at his station.

I wondered whether Mr. Plaintalk ever really watched some of the folks he had employed at his station perform. Of course he did, he knew. Just didn't make any difference.

Bottom line, I knew what I'd have to do.

Leave. Just like for college. Would have to leave Wichita to chase my dream.

I had one aunt known for stepping up to the plate who made a series of phone calls and found a voice coach for me via a local university. I met with him several times just to smooth the rough edges, polish my delivery. This professional didn't agree with Mr. Smooth Talk. I later found out that often professional broadcasters utilize voice coaches as do singers, actors, entertainers. Never have forgotten what this aunt did to boost to my confidence.

There were other disappointments in my search for a broadcasting job in Wichita. This led me to conclude that I needed to go to grad school and continue my education at the Master's level at a college affiliated with a major television station.

There were two in the Midwest, the University of Missouri at Columbia and Iowa State University. I applied and was admitted to both. I chose Iowa State because I could start the program sooner. Just as important ... I could get out of Wichita much quicker. And that's exactly what I did.

Day 13
Jack Shelley, Iowa State and WOI-TV: 1979–81 (Ames/ Des Moines, Iowa)

A booming, larger than life figure, John "Jack" Shelley was a man legendary in Iowa news broadcasting. I met him as a first year graduate student at Iowa State University. In title he was my major professor, but he became much, much more. This compassionate man played a crucial role in my life.

Mr. Shelley's broadcasting career was long over when I met him in February, 1979; he had been a well respected member of the faculty since the mid-1960s. But what makes Mr. Shelley a standout in my life was that not only was he instrumental in opening the door to broadcasting for me, but he also was vital in renewing my faith in people.

Don't recall how many classes I took from him. He was tough but fair. His keen observations and reading of situations and people were, of course, spot on. Yet Professor Shelley, or "Jack" as he was known, did some things for me that no other educator had ever done before. Or since.

I've tried to emulate his ideology and thoughtfulness in my role as an educator, but my attempts fail miserably when compared to the efforts of this man. Mr. Shelley went well above and beyond the call of duty in working with young people. One person can make a vital difference in the failure or success of another.

Three examples follow.

I had been an Iowa State student for a while and had applied for and landed an assistantship working at the university-owned, commercially operated television station, WOI-5 TV. I wanted a slot as a student news reporter, responsible for weekend news stories, but I was assigned by the student supervisor, a fulltime Caucasian male anchor, to work inside the newsroom as a production assistant, i.e., a glorified "gopher." This person in this position did everything from running the teleprompter for anchors and rewriting short news stories to listening to the squawky radio scanner for police and fire calls. But, no on air television work.

This male anchor would "hire" or assign undergraduate male Caucasian students off the street and without much journalism experience -- less than the journalism experience that I had -- for on air reporting slots. I was trying to patiently wait my turn but after several months, it was quite frustrating.

Finally I voiced my frustration to professor Shelley.

He clearly understood and most importantly, empathized with my disappointment as he knew from the outset what my broadcast goal was and how well my hard work had prepared me for a broadcasting career. He didn't make any promises but just said he'd talk to the supervisor. And within a few days, just like that, after years of frustration I finally got the chance to be on air as a television news reporter. So what if it was as a student reporter, part-time only gig, on the weekend news team of the station that lagged well behind in the coveted Des Moines area ratings race. I was on the air! And it was due to Jack, nobody else.

In my follow up conversation with the news anchor he defensively claimed that he had "needed me inside" – off camera -- due to my maturity. Yeah, sure and there's a bridge for sale in New York. Couldn't buy that argument. There was always an experienced female anchor/news producer running the show as well as a very capable student news producer (also female).

Needless to say I took this opportunity very seriously.

But that wasn't all.

Later in my student career as I was preparing my Master's thesis, Mr. Shelley was always available for crystal clear direction and sound advice. He was a godsend in so many different ways, which leads me to another critical experience.

I had finished my coursework and completed my assistantship but I could not land a full-time job. I was forced to return, unfortunately, to Wichita. My thesis was still not completed but I could not afford to stay in Ames. I had hired a typist to make grammatical corrections and type the final draft. While I could mail the paper back and forth, this would have gotten expensive. Professor Shelley offered to pick up and/or deliver my paper to the typist. He didn't charge me for gas, travel, time, etc. He did it out of the kindness of his heart.

More than once this kind giant of a man already in his late 60's did my "leg work."

Thank God for Mr. Shelley.

But there's one additional thing that Jack did.

The thesis was done, and I was to return to campus for my oral exam in front of my committee. In telephone conversation Mr. Shelley told me to stop at WHO-TV in Des Moines before coming to Ames. This was the television station that he famously put on the map as a longtime broadcaster. Specifically I was to see the TV news director, Mr. Phil Thomas. Jack Shelley had previously mentioned he would talk to Mr. Thomas on my behalf.

So I stopped by the station, just as I was. Dressed in jeans and a sport shirt after a long drive from Wichita. I was as casual as I could be. I didn't stop to change clothing, to freshen up, nothing; I wasn't expecting anything after so many disappointments, so much prior rejection, doors not closed but nailed, if not sealed, tightly shut.

I'd returned home to Wichita, once again, this time armed with numerous resume tapes. I'd been sending out tapes for several months well before leaving Ames without success. To say I was, once again, frustrated, would be putting it lightly. This time, once again, I'd done everything I knew to do and I remembered the hard lessons learned after graduating from A.U. I applied for jobs, and sent tapes all over the country to medium and smaller broadcast markets where I thought I would have a legitimate shot. But all doors seemed to be closed (especially in Wichita). Was history repeating itself yet again?

En route to Ames by way of Des Moines I stopped by to see Mr. Thomas. He was not only familiar with my work but genuinely interested in me. Shock! Surprise! But there was more, a great deal more.

With a sincere, genuine gleam in his eyes Mr. Thomas offered me a television news reporting job!

Praise God! Finally! I had literally prayed for this moment. I'd made a "deal" with God and God came through—with Jack Shelley as his go-between! (Although in my naivete and ignorance I then tried to negotiate a higher starting salary! I cringe now at my youthful folly!).

Jack Shelley, a man who not only was a great teacher and mentor but also a kind, compassionate man. He was instrumental in making both my academic and professional dreams come true. I'm sure I wasn't the only one who could tell a wonderful Jack Shelley story. He passed long after I'd left on air broadcasting.

I will always hold the highest amount of respect and gratitude for this man and cherish his memory. John "Jack" Shelley, more than an outstanding broadcaster and teacher, an outstanding, caring man.

Day 14
Apartment Search: 1980 (Des Moines, Iowa)

"Reggie Jarrell, Newscenter 13." Had just taken my first, full time "dream" job as a television reporter at WHO-TV (thank you, Phil Thomas, for giving me that opportunity!), in Des Moines, Iowa and was looking for an apartment to rent. Was temporarily housed in a downtown hotel. This was well before the convenience of the internet. I found the apartment by scanning newspaper ads and following up by Ma Bell.

Didn't want to live in Des Moines proper if at all possible, but was looking for a place in either the suburbs or the outskirts of the city. After years of chasing my dream, I was excited about this TV reporting job finally becoming real, no longer a distant possibility.

I was quite familiar with Des Moines, Iowa, the state capital. Had relatives in the city including one of Pop's sisters, the lovely, joyful Aunt Willa Mae, and her longtime wonderful husband, the kind and friendly Uncle Floyd.

Ames, where I'd done graduate work, was about 25 or 30 easy interstate miles north of Des Moines. Felt comfortable with Des Moines, I felt at home.

I was also very familiar with the city from working as a weekend student reporter at WOI-TV, the commercial television station then owned and operated by Iowa State University. Story assignments would sometimes require a trip to Des Moines and I enjoyed those times hopping in the Channel 5 van news vehicle with a photographer and hitting the road.

I thought I was prepared and ready for this new adventure, which of course, began with the search for housing.

I had in mind a studio apartment, preferably, furnished. I really didn't want, or need, a one bedroom place as I was thinking of the problem of buying and moving furniture. Then there were utility and other bills and I was trying to keep expenses to a minimum.

My search began!

It didn't take long to run into a malady I was well aware of but not expecting in this time and place: that old toxic poison.

Why include this experience? Because my housing search was the very first time I'd ever tasted the rotten fruit of prejudice served in this particular manner.

I saw a newspaper ad and I phoned and made arrangements to go and see the vacant apartment in an hour or so. When I arrived I could see this really wasn't the type of place I was interested in as the curb appeal was severely lacking.

Didn't matter. Contacted the landlord's leasing agent, a middle-aged Caucasian woman.

The woman said the place was rented. Already? Couldn't be, that quickly. I'd just talked to her, or somebody, on the phone. But I knew what game she was playing when I first laid eyes on her, or alternatively, when she laid eyes on me. Might not be able to judge a book by its cover but faces and eyes don't lie. Her rigid features and hardened eyes told me her story.

Didn't argue with the woman as I didn't care. Didn't want to live there anyway, but I thought as a reporter this would make an ideal subject for an exposé on subtle racism, discriminatory actions in supposedly "public" accommodations.

Went to another apartment complex the same day. This "garden apartment," i.e., basement level, was located in one of the western suburbs of the city. The complex featured a sole building on the east side of a somewhat busy street. The location was OK but the building's exterior pea green color was just plain and simple ugly. This same color scheme extended to the interior walls of the apartment.

I didn't care for that color. Couldn't see myself getting up from bed, or coming home, looking at those slimy, vomit colored walls. Yes, it was that bad. Unfortunately there was more.

The landlord, another woman, was friendly enough as she showed me the place. She was informative enough, perhaps too informative. She pointed out that I might not be comfortable there because of one particular resident... Don't remember the details but she made it clear that although I was free to rent the apartment, my neighbor would not be welcoming.

Now I could take that one of two ways: one, the landlord was lying and it wasn't the neighbor but the management who wasn't welcoming and didn't want an integrated building, or, two, she was being truthful, trying to be helpful in issuing the warning.

I thought, however, if in fact a resident was a racist, I had as much right to the peaceful enjoyment of the premises as they did. If there was a problem the landlord had the obligation to at least attempt to keep the peace.

A bit naïve in my thinking but then again while I had encountered racism and discrimination before, I had yet to learn that in many instances in the good ole U.S. of A. the predominant and default attitude, much too often, is to maintain and sustain the status quo. And that usually means to the benefit of the most powerful to the detriment of the least powerful.

Didn't have to think long about that place; even if everything had been hunky dory, I still would not have wanted to look at, or live within, those offensive, putrid green walls.

Thus I resumed my search but my adventure didn't last long. The third place I found was a multi-building complex with white buildings trimmed in black in Urbandale, another west Des Moines suburb, and I knew when I first saw it, this was it! This was the place for me, I felt comfortable and at home just walking around the place that first time. Like a worn, comfortable old shoe, it felt like a good fit. Walked into the management office, no problem, no games, no antics. Looked at an available studio apartment, a second story very modern unit with a balcony, a lovely carpet, a large Murphy bed that folded into the wall, and all the other amenities one would expect.

And the price was right!

Wonderful! My adventure was just beginning, in more ways than one.

Day 15
SUNO & African Students: 1983-84 (New Orleans, Louisiana)

Parents send their children to college for a plethora of reasons: to grow academically, to mature, for exposure to different people, to get out of the house. Probably for most the bottom line is to prepare for a better future, career, job, higher income. For international students, in general, the stakes can be extremely high with students leaving home and country for an extended time period with few, if any, guarantees.

One would like to think that although the college campus is just a small microcosm of the general society, at least in the hallowed halls of higher education students can escape, even if just for a while, many of the perils that rip the spirit and crush dreams. One would like to entertain the notion that within the ivory towered walls a student can expect to get a fair shake for much of the time.

Usually, based on observations and experience, that is so.

But not always.

And when one is caught in the blinding gaze of unfairness, injustice, and ignorance on the college campus, one quickly realizes the cost of higher education taxes not only the purse strings but also, and more importantly, the very heart and soul.

Even of the young.

And that realization just intensifies the pain.

His name escapes me but his experience doesn't.

He had a quiet, polite persona and a large Afro crowned his head. Like his fellow international students, this African student was serious and diligent in his study. He was a student in one of my college print journalism classes in New Orleans, and he was having some serious troubles. I knew one of the college's key administrators could help.

"Why don't you go and talk to Dr.____," I mildly suggested, knowing that this vice president, a campus power broker, could provide essential information, if not outright assistance, for this top-of-the-class student.

I was caught off guard by the student's response. What started as a promising, engaging interaction suddenly transformed into a somber exchange with a cold, dark shadow.

What was happening here?

There was no response from the student. His once spirit-filled eyes were now downcast and heavy, reflecting pain and hurt. I just didn't understand.

Dr. ___ could help, I thought. He had the authority, power and capability to ease this young man's suffering, I knew it!

The student politely excused himself while expressing appreciation for my time.

Problem resolved, I thought, dismissing the confusing interaction and moving on.

Fast forward to sometime later. I was engaged in conversation with this same administrator I had recommended to my African student. We were discussing school related issues and students when this longtime college administrator, the second in command at this campus, with an earned doctorate and years of experience, made an unforgettable, alarming declaration.

"I don't like African students," he stated just as smoothly as one would say they disliked apple pie or grape soda. "They don't pay their bills."

To say shock registered in my mind is putting it lightly. To make such a prejudiced statement to another educator on the grounds of an institution of higher learning! It not only indicated arrogance and conceit, but a frightening level of ignorance and elitism.

In that moment I realized the reason for the student's trepidation and why he looked so weary and rejected.

I didn't understand then, but in this moment with this college official I clearly understood.

The student knew there would be no help from that administrator, and most likely no help from this school in which he had placed his educational investment.

This student knew what I'd just learned: The scales are supposed to be even, balanced and fair, but for these students they were not. Many cards were stacked against them. And in this game there was little chance of winning.

You see this African student was a very long distance from home. He had limited financial resources and a small support system. Here he was an undergraduate student attending an historically black college and the administrator in question was an African American man.

With a heart of stone and ice running through his veins.

Are we not our brother's keeper?

Day 16
The Parade: 1988-90 (Quad Cities, Illinois/Iowa)

Don't know how I found out about the Labor Day Parade, whether it was from a newspaper, television ad or what but I thought it would be a nice event for our two small sons. It was not held in Davenport, the community in which we lived, but in one of the neighboring cities that bordered the Mississippi River and was part of the Quad-Cities (even if that moniker was misleading as there were actually six to eight communities on both sides of the river). It was the late 1980s.

I looked forward with great anticipation to the day's festivities and made sure to get to the parade route well before the crowds to get a prime spot. Found the perfect one on the edge of the street just off the curb. Didn't want anything or anyone to block or even partially obstruct our view. Wasn't concerned about me or the wife but wanted to make sure that the boys, about six and four years of age, wouldn't have any problem seeing. Wanted them to have a positive experience.

To further set the stage I must add that our boys were not rambunctious, push and shove, grab and shove children. While certainly playful, they were polite, mild mannered, respectful. Although of course I was biased, they were wonderful boys.

The smaller community-oriented parade begins! Here we go! A marching band with horns a blarin', drums a blasting and feet a stompin' comes sashaying by. Oh here's a float and what's that? Somebody throwing candy at children along the parade route – an added treat! Here it comes! A handful of candy being pitched this way -- that way! Children hastily scampering for the sugary sweet treasures landing near their feet!

Okay, none tossed our way – but that's all right! Here comes another group with more candy raining down almost like pennies from heaven. But that rain of candy dries up when it nears our children.

Hey something is going on here! It is so clear that even blind Bartimaeus could see how unholy, hateful, and downright sinful some of these people are. Time after time when those parade participants pass our way they toss no candy, no trinkets, no nothing in the area where our boys are standing. Even when parade marchers, old and young, all Caucasian, stroll by handing out goodies, they conveniently don't see our children and strut past our boys. It is noticeable and obvious. And painful. This is not what I expected, not at all.

Could it be because we were the only African Americans in that area?

Oh, here come some people dressed in blue uniforms, the garb of the United States Post Office. Surely someone in this group will exercise common decency. I get my hopes up. Surely someone in this group is color blind and will share their treats with us.

My oldest son has also noticed what is going on, how he and his little brother are being ignored time and time again.

"Daddy why won't they give us any candy?" he innocently asks, the bewilderment etched in his puzzled eyes.

I make up some excuse to rationalize and hide the ignorance, cruelty and hard hearts we are witnessing. The blatant racism.

"You'll get some, the parade is not over," I tell the six-year-old, hoping I'm speaking the truth but ever so aware that people, adults and even children, can be cruel without reason.

They walk on by carrying their bags full of candy but exercising very selective sight and even more selective giving. Should I have really been surprised? Isn't that the way it too often is in this good old U.S. of A? At any and all levels. Wherever there are so called "opportunities." In jobs, education, salaries, housing, services – even when children seek to participate in a community parade.

Back to the parade. Unfortunately, these US Post Office workers suffer from the same sickening malady that afflicts the other parade participants. They too walk up to and right on past the boys, disregarding their pleading eyes, leaving our sons' palms still wide open and their small hands empty.

This blatant disregard for little children, MY children. Pathetic. Senseless. Evil.

I am more than a little perturbed. If I'd only known this would happen, I never would have given this penny ante parade the slightest thought.

About ready to go home and the boys still have zilch, not a single soul has shared anything.

I am not just disappointed but disgusted. So much for this "community" parade.

What is this? I see very calculated, determined movement that catches my eye. A parade official or someone who looks to have something to do with the event is crossing the four lane street. The parade is still continuing, but he is walking through it. He is actually walking toward us. What is this?

This middle-aged Caucasian man crosses the street, looking directly at us, well actually, looking at the boys. Not only have our two small boys noticed the slight but so has this man. This stranger boldly steps to our boys. Ignoring the other surrounding children he gives our sons several trinkets and candy. He has seen what has happened and clearly he wants to right the very hurtful wrong. He gives sincerely, graciously to our boys. We appreciate it. I thank him.

We leave. We are thankful for this lone expression of grace, an unforgettably kind gesture that contrasts with our agonizing experience of ignorance, disrespect and prejudice.

Post Script. Thanks, but no thanks. We don't need the aggravation. We will never again attend another Labor Day or any other community sponsored holiday parade. Keep your hard candy and cheap plastic trinkets; I know where the store is.

The next parade we attend is years later. It was for Halloween and organized by an integrated, community social service agency where the director and founder was African American. One of our children participated -- as a high school student in the late 1990s. Candy and other free trinkets were not an issue then.

Teenagers could care less.

Day 17
Stranger, Coach, Mentor, Friend – Jerry Goodmon, Sr.: 1970-2022 (Wichita)

Do you remember the precise time and place that you met a best friend? Those moments stand out, cemented in our memories as life highlights. While struggling with bias and racism, a person needs a mentor, a friend, a confidant to help sooth ruffled feathers and calm nerves. Someone to help lower the internal thermostat, to keep you from exploding.

We see the evidence of that every day, folk exploding. Bias. Prejudice. Racism. Oppression. Unfairness. All will make you explode.

Not good for the heart. Not good for your health. Not good, period.

You need a friend.

Sometimes you find friends in the most unusual places, at unexpected times. Of course, at the time you don't know that this stranger will be anything more. Life surprises us. That's how I met someone who went from stranger, to acquaintance, coach, mentor, and friend, a friend who remained trustworthy, faithful and inspirational through many lifetime valleys and mountaintops, educational journeys, sports achievements, graduations, marriages, births, and of course, deaths. Someone who was a man of several titles, from coach, to principal, to Doctor, among others.

It was the early 1970s and I was in either 8th or 9th grade. My junior high school track team at Mayberry Junior High had a track meet at West High School. I was a sprinter, running the 100 and 220 yard dashes as well as a member of some of our relay teams.

Standing somewhere on the West High track field, near the long jump and pole vault area, I noticed and then struck up a conversation with a young black man who was a coach at West, Jerry Goodmon, Sr. I remember being impressed -- *Hey, there's a black coach here.* He was so personable and friendly. Short and stocky he had the build of a former football player, which he was. He just stood out. I looked forward to attending West and perhaps getting to know this man.

And that's exactly what happened. I became a freshman at West, tried out for the sophomore football team, my first attempt at playing organized team football, and Goodmon was my football coach my first year in high school. He was tough, but fair. He was complimentary, but challenging. He had high expectations, but he treated his athletes with respect. I started at one of the running back positions on Coach Goodmon's team, a highlight of my year.

In the spring track season I went out for the track team. And Coach Goodmon was the coach in charge of the "sprinters," those running the 100 and 220 yard dashes. Once again found myself under his tutelage and our relationship began slowly to develop, increasing in trust and confidence.

It was just something about the man. I dropped by his home and met his family. These visits were the building blocks of friendship. While I was in high school Coach Goodmon transitioned into education administration and became one of several vice principals at West High School.

West High had its share of racial incidents during the early 1970s and from time to time something would happen to poke the bear. Some confrontation or assault between African Americans and Caucasian students, either on or off campus, would result in tension and rioting among the students. Goodmon played a large role in handling those incidents, calming students, being present both as a listener and an advocate for all students, but especially for black students, making sure that we were treated fairly. Often Goodmon could be found right in the middle of a conflict, pulling up his sleeves and getting in the midst of the chaos to stop the violence. A time or two, I was there and I saw him.

This was a man who wasn't afraid to get involved.

In my senior year I found myself needing his help due to problems with my journalism teacher. I worked on the school newspaper and although things had been fine between us, there came a time that I realized she was treating me differently than the Caucasian students. The rules were slightly altered, the procedures adjusted, issues handled differently.

Sometimes unfairly.

Example. Several West High students attended a high school journalism camp for two or three days at a small Kansas college shortly before school started my senior year. The boys were housed in one dorm, the girls in another. My roommate was another African American West student and the adjacent dorm room housed two Caucasian West students. One night we overheard those two white students talking and heard my name.

"Oh Reggie, that n***" -- just as plain as day.

Didn't count those two as friends but this certainly shed light on their perception of me. No, I didn't confront them, although I did think about it. But I did tell the journalism teacher, Mrs. Z.

Her response? Not much. Those things just happen. No big deal. To my knowledge, Mrs. Z said nor did absolutely nothing to the offenders. Certainly if she did, it never resulted in any type of apology or punishment.

And there's more. It was the usual practice that a senior would serve as editor of the student paper for a specific term, usually nine weeks. Because I was playing football again, I agreed to serve as editor after the football season. I knew I would not have sufficient time or energy to play football and serve as editor at the same time.

However the student who was supposed to be editor during football season could not. And Mrs. Z demanded that I step in.

Demanded. No compromise. No consideration of the prior agreement we had reached. It was then or never.

It felt unfair. She would not listen and did not care. My situation was less important than the other student's. I was "less than."
I served but what I feared would happen, did happen. Mrs. Z was quite, lets says, unhappy with the result. I was unhappy with the conditions. Anyone with eyes should have been able to see what was going on.

My solution: Drop the course and disengage from anything to do with journalism class, the newspaper and Mrs. Z. It hurt to do this. I hated to leave journalism. But I had grown tired of her mistreatment and her clouded view.

Once again I sought help from Coach Goodmon. He understood and stepped in. Mrs. Z didn't like that, but Coach, by then Assistant Principal Goodmon, got involved and helped me just when I needed it.

Across the years through college, marriage, law school I would drop in and talk with him. Spent many days during his later years sitting in his comfortable den, talking about all kinds of things: the past, West High, religion, sports, politics, family, and, of course, education (he had earned a Ph.D and offered considerable advice to me during my various graduate studies). We spent many hours just shooting the breeze and I thoroughly enjoyed every moment spent in his company.

His health began to fail and he knew it, but there was never a pity party, nor any "why me?" lamentations. He remained true to himself and true to others. Strong, faithful, encouraging, and loving until the end. Dr. Goodmon's final chapter was written in the fall, 2017.

Stranger. Acquaintance. Coach. Mentor. Dr. Goodmon blessed many students in so many different ways over the years.

He blessed me by being my friend. Rest well, Doc, for you have earned and richly deserve your eternal reward.

Day 18
The Judge: 1987-88 (Rock Island, Illinois)

I was standing near my office supervisor, the managing attorney, as she talked with the presiding judge during the "walk in" session at the small Illinois county courthouse. A walk in court was a designated time when short or simple matters could be presented before a judge.

Sometimes there were hearings, even "minor" contested hearings but that was not the norm. I was still learning the ropes, the tricks of the trade, as it was early in my legal career.

The broad faced judge with sleepy eyes had been on the bench for many years. He was middle aged, with a grandfatherly, calm demeanor. He was being "informed" of "the black letter law" by my supervisor.

The black letter law. One local area attorney was notorious for advertising his services by stressing that the law was not black and white but shades of gray, which implied there was some discretion allowed. Sometimes.

But there are areas of law that are crystal clear, or strictly speaking, written in black and white -- if such and such happens, then so and so is the consequence. In short, there is no discretion.

Such was the situation in this particular case before the court. Our managing attorney was skilled in both interpretation and application of the law in question. He stood before Judge Grandfather showing the judge the black letter law as published in the Illinois Revised Statutes.

I could not believe what I heard. Shocked was putting it mildly.

"I'm not going to do that!" Grandfatherly Judge declared empathically. "You can look for another judge, but I'm not going to do that!"

What is this? A judge, when shown what the black letter law requires, absolutely refusing to "do that!" And on top of that, defying the law in front of any and all who could hear him!

He was encouraging judge shopping.

Well, well. Doesn't that beat all?

The managing attorney was more than a little annoyed and frustrated. Fit to be tied. Disgusted. A look of exasperation as she walked past me going to search for another judge.

This was all still new to me. We never discussed this type of situation in law school. What do you do when a judge flat out refuses to follow the black letter law? What do you do when the judge explicitly states that not only will he not follow the law, but the attorney can go search for another judge? This is not a rhetorical situation but a real live, flesh and blood case with consequences for people's lives.

That brief exchange quickly opened my eyes to the reality of the justice system; some people will get to do only what they want to do regardless of whether it is just, or fair, or equitable, or reasonable, or moral, or ethical, or yes, even legal.

Surely that's not the way the justice system really works? Or is it?

Ask the Judge.

Just don't hold your breath waiting for an honest answer.

Day 19
Walking Diamond: 1988-91 (Davenport, Iowa)

Who knew walking a tiny dog could turn into a potentially dangerous racial incident?

It was a pleasant summer Saturday evening. Our three small children had been put to bed and it was my task to walk our tiny, black-with-white-streaks terrier. Diamond came to us as a pup from someone who worked in another social service agency in the Martin Luther King Center building in Rock Island. That was also the home of my then employer. The children named her Diamond because of a jeweled shaped white spot in the center of her forehead above her eyes. Cute little thing she was.

We lived in a gray, two story side-by-side duplex on a block of similarly colored, and shaped, duplexes. We were acquainted with a few of our neighbors in this integrated neighborhood and our children's playmates were other youngsters in this area. They and we got along well with everyone.

Although we shared the front and rear yard with our neighbor on the other side of our duplex, a mother with two biracial children, we stayed on our side of our unit. Nice, quiet family. In the rear our yards bordered the grounds of an elementary school, providing plenty of room – and grass – for the little ones, to play, roam, and explore.

And plenty of areas to walk Diamond to relieve herself.

Across the street in front of us was also a huge vacant, unfinished lot that extended a block or two, maybe even more.

Another prime area to walk the dog.

Thus on this warm, sunny eve that was precisely what I decided to do, walk Diamond in the lot across the street, which I'd frequently done. We had church the next day and my mind was on Sunday things-to-do.

Diamond was leashed and we had crossed the street in front of our duplex onto the vacant lot. No one else was on the sidewalk, in the lot, or anywhere in sight. Peace and quiet. Alone with my thoughts, and Diamond.

Then out of the blue, breaking into my peaceful ascent into solemn bliss, I heard a voice from behind me yelling from a passing vehicle.

"I wish I had a n*** to walk!"

Those sharp, piercing, iron-like words exploded into my consciousness. Akin to the wind being knocked out of me, being stabbed in the back and slapped into a racist reality, I questioned myself.

Did I hear what I think I heard? No – no – no, couldn't be! Seemed like time stood still. But the respite was brief. And like a hard slap in the face a second time these words from a stranger polluted not only the air, but my very being.

Yep, he had the audacity to repeat his vile words.

"I wish I had a n*** to walk."

I turned to see the man who assailed me stepping from a pickup truck that had parked in the driveway of the duplex next to ours. He did not live in the unit as the tenant he visited was a single parent Caucasian woman, middle aged, with a small, very young elementary aged child. We knew the woman and had never had any problems with her. We were separated by the unit which housed our mutual neighbor, the single parent mom with the biracial children.

And just like that, the racist escaped into the confines of his prejudice, hiding behind not only the screen and the entry doors of the duplex, but hiding behind the doors of his ignorance and bigotry.

It wasn't so simple for me.

My very first thought was, "let it go." Just "let it go."

Really? "Let it go."

But I couldn't, not this time. Anger and rage started to boil within me and my second thought was vastly different.

"This ain't the 1950's" I thought. A time when so many Black people were subject to every kind of injustice, oppression and mistreatment imaginable. Explicit and implicit. Overt and covert. Personal, cultural, systematic, institutional, legal.

And of course, unfortunately, violent.

Maybe you have even seen some of those photos.

Black victims of lynching. Often men, but also women and children too.

Often surrounded by mass crowds of Caucasian folks, sometimes with smug smiles, always with hard, cold eyes celebrating their accomplishment, posing proudly with their lifeless victims, evidence of their victory, as hunters with stalked trophies.

No – no – no!

"This ain't the 1950's" started to ring endlessly through my mind.

And my anger, my rage intensified.

I went back into my duplex and told my spouse what happened. Didn't have to say much. She could see the rage in my eyes. Afterwards, she told me my eyes were blood red. A look she very rarely had witnessed during our relationship. That rage I'd long worked to keep hidden.

To keep buried.

To keep confined.

I continued to pace throughout the first floor of our unit as I talked with my wife. Back and forth. Restless. Anxious. Angry. Excited. Then I'd stepped outside and, being careful to stay on the sidewalk, walked over to the front of duplex where the bigot escaped. I paced in front of the duplex, but he wouldn't show his face. He wouldn't open the door. He wouldn't do anything.

He wouldn't but I will.

He's hiding like an animal in a hole.

Then I went for Old Betsy. He wouldn't want to tangle with Old Betsy. Old Betsy was my extremely short barreled 12-gauge shotgun that I had the tendency to carry in the trunk of my car. I'd purchased Old Betsy when I was a college student having problems with another student and kept her in my dorm closet.

And now Old Betsy was back in my hands. But there was a problem, the gun was not loaded. I usually kept it unloaded to force myself to take a cooling down, reflection period if necessary. I know me and it was best if I kept the shells out of the gun. Unless…

And this was an "unless" situation. Or so I thought.

So that was a big problem; Old Betsy was unloaded. But there was another big problem: I was so angry I could not remember where I put the shells!

You see it was Pop who taught me to hunt and shoot as a pre-teen. And he taught me Rule #1 was essential: If and when there is a problem with another person, "Never show an unloaded gun."

For obvious reasons. The other person, the problem person,

wouldn't know and if he too had a gun then...

I am in a rage. I have my gun with no shells but I know I cannot go outside with the gun unloaded.

Decided to call the police. Got a dispatcher. Clearly she did not want to be bothered. Didn't think much of my situation. Dismissive. Minimizing. Not important. Attitudes of privilege and entitlement.

"We don't come out for neighborhood disputes like that."

What? I am telling the dispatch there is a problem and this dispatcher is clearly pooh-poohing my feelings? This is not the type of problem they address?

"All right then. But if something happens don't say that I didn't call you and try to get help, understand?"

And then the tone of the dispatcher changed.

"No, no, don't do anything. A car will be right out."

I am still in a rage, still holding Old Betsy, and I ask my wife to call a dear friend, a deacon from our church, to come over and talk with me. I recognize I need help.

Deacon lives nearby and he comes. And we talk. He stays.

And the police come, take a report and go over to the duplex. Racist Redneck still won't answer the door. Cops run his plates. They "know" him. He's had some legal problems, they say. Perhaps that's the reason he won't open the door. They spend some time there, come back to visit with me, then leave.

My deacon friend stays. Most of the night. Literally. Finally I settle down. Old Betsy is put away.

I go to church the next day and apologize to the congregation. One preacher tabs me with the moniker: "Rev. Shotgun." Clearly it could have turned violent. Could have been very destructive. Destroyed my family. Destroyed my life.

Could see the headlines in the local paper:

LOCAL LAWYER, PREACHER SHOOTS MAN OVER RACIAL SLUR

No, the stakes were too high and the pain and agony would have been unfathomable.

But it could have happened. Unfortunately. Although I was just out, minding my own business, walking a tiny dog.

How many other black folk have been victimized while minding their own business?

Only God knows.

What if I had found the shotgun shells?

I found them the next day. My wife knew where they were all the time, including that Saturday night, but she wasn't telling.

Calmer heads prevailed. Wife. Deacon.

And the next evening: Diamond and I went back across the street for our walk.

Quiet all right but no peace. No solitude. That realm of innocence shattered.

P.S. Never saw Paul Prejudice again, he never reappeared at the duplex. And I looked.

Yet I clearly saw how God was in this thing, every step of the way. God protects us, as the saying goes, from dangers seen and unseen. From others. Sometimes protects us even from ourselves.

Day 20
Prairie State – Mr. Man: 1990-92 (Rock Island, Illinois)

I had been an attorney working for a legal services organization for several years. Had seen and heard all kinds of things, unusual things from all extremes, both in and outside the courthouse. But one experience with a racist shed light on just how color coded the legal system is for certain folks of entitlement and privilege.

Was minding my own business, in my own world, working at a desk in the reception area of our Rock Island, Illinois legal services office. Don't remember why I was sitting there instead of in my own, windowless but comfortable office among a cluster of five or six other interior offices. Yet there I was at one of several desks in our secretary/receptionist's office area.

Suddenly I looked up and watched the forty-something casually attired Caucasian man strolling through the outside door into our office like he owned the place.

Dropping a small stack of papers onto the desk facing me, this Mr. Man whispered under his breath, "Here, n***!" His voice was pitched low, ever so careful so no other ears would capture the foul stench of his nasty words.

And just as quickly as he entered, he turned and slithered out of the door.

I was stunned. Shocked. Astonished. Amazed at his hubris.

Mr. Man was the defendant in an elder domestic violence abuse case and I represented his grandfather. There were not just one or two but a series of alleged incidents.

Mr. Man was apparently reared by his grandparents. His mother lived in town.

Well known within the legal community. Time and again Mr. Man found himself on the wrong side of the civil law. Mr. Man insisted on representing himself in court. The judges, bailiffs, court reporters, court clerks as well as the police all knew who and what he was. He was often seen in the county courthouse library doing research.

More than just a thorn in the side, more than just a nuisance, to some he was a reoccurring nightmare. To others, a living, notorious, irritating cancer.

And a devout, overt racist. Period.

But due to his color, heritage and background of societal privilege and entitlement, Mr. Man was allowed to assert, even vent, his legal rights in the court system.

More than once. Thus he gained a less than stellar reputation.

Don't remember how I ended up assigned to represent his grandfather in obtaining an order of protection (a restraining order) but I found myself on the receiving end of his verbal diatribes. We had obtained the initial order, called an "emergency" order, without court or legal notice to the defendant, as is allowed in certain cases.

The emergency order, signed by a judge, was effective for a maximum of 14 days during which the order, and other legal documents, served as notice to the defendant of the legal proceedings. Upon service of this order, the court had the authority to issue a two-year order of protection. However, the defendant could appear to contest this order and/or request a trial.

In short, not only could the defendant be prohibited from inflicting additional abuse, the defendant could be ordered to stay away from the home.

Domestic violence, of course, includes elder abuse.

I handled many of these cases and a few stand out. I remember many clients, generally women, being deathly afraid of their perpetrators. Some of these abusers were dangerous, very dangerous.

Mr. Man was certainly a danger to his grandparents, and it was clear that intimidation and threats were included in his arsenal of abuse.

And I saw, up close and personal, the extent of his maliciousness.

He had the reputation among those in legal circles of having some mental issues, being delusional and psychotic.

His angry, hostile outbursts directed toward me, before, during and after the court proceedings showed me his bold and aggressive behavior in public.

What astounded me was how often he was allowed to spray his toxic venom.

People heard him, even judges. I don't recall any rebukes or admonitions.

I remember telling Mother how mentally unstable he was and how crazy he behaved.

Mother asked a poignant question.

"Did he say anything to the judge?"

"No, he didn't."

"Well he's not too crazy."

Uh huh.

So many appeared to look the other way, for whatever reason.

Often I thought about how quick the legal establishment was to silence a black person for even the slightest trace of what Mr. Man did. Or said.

From inside the system I saw a double standard.

But I had to simply endure, go through the process, with all of his overt and insidious attention-grabbing antics.

What all did he say? I don't remember. I repressed those other memories.

But I do remember feeling attacked, insulted, abused, angry, and more by the language he used with me. Wishing for vengeance.

What happened?

Mr. Man got his court hearing, as was his legal right.

It went on for an entire day. A judge. A court reporter. At least one bailiff in a courtroom. Precious legal resources. You get the picture.

An all-day event where he was allowed to play lawyer.

It need not and should not have gone that long. Yet it did. Mr. Man went on and on and had a captive audience.

Mr. Man was also noted for filing *pro se* appeals to the appellate court. Knowing that when he filed another one of his pointless, resource draining receptacles of verbosity, it would go nowhere.

But for those sucked into this process, dealing with his hostile and aberrant attitude was an exercise in patience and frustration.

The bottom line was we obtained the plenary order of protection that day.

After a seemingly agonizing process, the case was closed and I was done. As expected, Mr. Man continued his legal mumble jumble for another day.

But honestly he did start to get on my nerves. I had to exercise due care, extreme care, not to drown in his ignorance or be consumed by his foolishness.

You see I knew where Mr. Man lived. I drove by his house more than once. Checking it out.

Yet that isn't the way. Regardless. Do the right thing. Hold on.

This experience supplied yet another hard lesson in life.

There are inalienable rights that include freedom of speech. But there is also something called privilege that far too often allows some people to manipulate the courts.

Privilege. For some.

Day 21
The College President: 1997-98 (Quad Cities)

"No, he didn't!"
Perhaps my eyes narrowed, my steely gaze a slim glint staring ahead, a deep crevice burrowed in my forehead. Tension. Disbelief. Shock. Surprise.
But really, what should I have expected?

I added another career when I joined the faculty of a university in Iowa. Another venue for life lessons.
It was the final time I sat in the university President's impressive, expansive office. After teaching at the small, religiously-affiliated Midwestern college for six years (tenure had been granted after only three years, I'd had enough. Enough lies, deception and manipulation. Enough of the university's false front of racial sensitivity and liberalism. Enough of the covert, subtle racist underpinnings in the infrastructure of that well known regional institution.
I had gone through the process seeking promotion to the rank of associate professor and had been denied by a committee of professors led by the university's second in command, the vice president or provost. This man had a distinctive southern drawl suggesting his southern roots.
I was the sole black assistant professor among a handful of black professionals employed there. One brother had dual teaching and administrative duties but I was the lone black full-time teacher at this urban school of about 2500 students in eastern Iowa.
I was not the first, but it had been many years since my predecessor had served as the trail blazer for black faculty.
My application for promotion to associate professor was denied during the initial application process and was denied again after the subsequent appeal, a process that occurred over the course of 1 1/2 to

2 academic years as I recall. I was actually told to apply again, a third time. Thanks but no thanks. I was clear it was time to cut my losses.

Initially I felt positive in seeking the promotion. I had the full support of my immediate supervisor, the college Dean, a kind, very personable, excellent scholar who had hired me. I did not, however, have the support of my department head, who undermined my application for reasons that, in hindsight, were indicative of the elitist, arrogant attitude of some in the administration.

At the beginning, as in most of my other professional associations, I was hopeful and optimistic.

I approached this college while I was employed at a local newspaper. After months of discussion a job description developed and an offer was made. The position specifically was created for me although it was advertised. The position included dual responsibilities: teacher of communications and administrator of the school's multicultural (i.e., black) program, which supposedly had, a small budget for programming and activities.

And that's where the problem started. A nonexistent program with an invisible budget.

I am still waiting to get that check. Any check for the multicultural program.

After being hired I found it increasingly difficult to access any of the supposed program funds for any reason. Not even for a pizza party for students or a packet of thumb tacks for a bulletin board.

I can't remember how much the supposed budget consisted of, whether it was $100, $1000 or even $10,000, but I never received one cent of the promised money. Despite requests, nothing.

The funds were supposedly available, but something always pre-empted them. In other words it was a front, a straw or dummy program which existed only on paper. The campus -- meaning faculty, staff, and students -- assumed it was a viable, living program, but a few of us, the handful of black professionals on campus, actually knew the hard truth.

After several years of frustration I resigned that part of my position. I was just window dressing, a token held up so the powers that be could say, "we have a diverse faculty...."

Another educational employment opportunity where I had been deceived and lied to. This wasn't the first time but this, in my eyes, was worse than before because these folk were supposed to be Christians.

So I concentrated on my teaching (I had earned tenure and more about that later. Another substantial incident occurred that was part of the backstory to the promotion debacle and that caused my perception to change. For the worse. A slap in the face. A kick in the behind. Or perhaps my perception cleared as my eyes were pried open.

After teaching communications and media courses for several years, I was assigned a new course to teach. There was no consultation with my department head, no request for my input. I was simply told I would teach a seminar called radio production and a lab. The last time I'd had worked with radio or audio production techniques was twenty-some years earlier. As a student at Baker University in Baldwin City, Kansas, in the mid-1970s I did a stint as a weekly disc jockey at the college radio station. My professional experience was in television and print journalism. Regardless I was assigned to teach radio production.

I should have immediately gone to the department head and made my discomfort with this assignment known, but I did not. I wanted to be a team player and do the best I could. Thus I planned to seek help from the wonderful staff person who served as the campus radio station manager and audio producer. I would grin and bear it, figure out a way to make it work.

But, apparently, I made a serious mistake in judgment.

By way of background, I have been in many different classrooms across the years, both as teacher and student. I always appreciated those teachers who were open, honest, and transparent, especially about their shortcomings, weaknesses, and failures. It made them seem like real, approachable people. Especially those law school professors.

On the first day of radio production class at this university I thought I would do what I'd seen and heard other instructors do with my students. So to the 15 to 20 students in class I revealed my background was not in production but pledged I would make it work so that they would get what they needed to be successful with the subject matter.

So much for transparency. So much for being open and honest.

I forgot that the rules of the game are different for some of us.

I forgot that our experiences and qualifications are still suspect by some.

I forgot where I was.

Some students didn't appreciate my disclosure of the weak links in my background. A group of students, not sure exactly how many, went to the President's office and complained about my lack of experience to teach that class.

The complaint filtered down through the various levels and the Dean brought it to my attention. The solution: the production lab component would be taught by the radio station manager previously mentioned. The students got the instruction and experience with the radio/audio equipment and everything else they needed.

This incident apparently was pivotal in the denial of my application for promotion years later. This single class, this single group of complaints. Regardless of all the other classes, all the other students, all the other positive student evaluations.

Despite earning tenure in my third year, a milestone. None of that mattered to certain folks on the promotions committee. Perhaps there was more to it?

After going through the denial of promotion the Dean made a telling statement.

"Just because you don't eat lunch in the faculty dining room shouldn't make any difference. So what?"

To the "powers that be" the token wasn't "seen" enough. I wasn't playing the political public relations game.

That was true. But the meals in the faculty dining hall weren't free. Money was tight in the family with children in school and participating in various activities: Cub Scouts, Brownies, musical instruments for band or orchestration, fees for soccer, YMCA basketball, dance class, etc. During this time I had also taken on other jobs -- writing free lance columns for *The Rock Island Argus Moline Dispatch* newspaper company; teaching alternately at two community colleges, Scott Community College in Iowa and Blackhawk College in Illinois. Oh, and for a few months working part time as a janitor in an office/small factory building until I developed health problems due to some of the fumes in the building. There was good reason to eat at my desk and work while I ate.

Across the years there always seemed to be something off with that university job, something not quite right. I sensed something seductive yet hazardous. Something was amiss.

That led to periods of disgust, disappointment, frustration. And there were other incidents that made it clear I could not stay and live out my days in that situation. I simply could not see investing more time, more of my life in that environment, being treated as a token rather than part of a team. I had worked about six years at that school. Met some wonderful folk there, but the overall experience was distasteful.

A bitter taste lingered in my mouth and an ache in my stomach from layers of prejudice, bias, discrimination wrapped in a sandwich of oppression, marginalization and rejection.

Presence without power. Disparate treatment. Glass (more like cement ceiling.

And besides, the money wasn't that good.

Thus I found myself in the President's office, for a final meeting. Call it hubris but I felt, after all this, I was owed a conversation, recognition of how I had been treated, and compensation. Of course, legal action had crossed my mind many times but after all, this was a religious institution and I am a minister. How would that look? Airing that dirty laundry just didn't seem to be the moral, ethical, proper, or Christian thing to do.

So I went to the President. You never know until you ask. The squeaky wheel gets the grease. And all the other platitudes. You never know.

I requested compensation. A severance package. Something. Far-fetched, of course.

I knew these people. Wasn't born yesterday. But I made my case. And the President, a sixty-something, six foot plus, huge, burly bear of a man with a propensity for hugging people claimed he understood. He said more.

"I want to do that," he said enthusiastically. I took it as a show of good faith appreciation of my services rendered. Wasn't prepared for what happened next. Didn't see it coming.

I was sitting down at a large table in the president's office. The conversation was cordial, polite. The President approached, standing next to me. Then quickly, like a scene from a 1930's movie, he lifted his huge paw and patted me on my head.

Like an adult pats a small toddler.

Like a child pats a dog.

I was shocked at this blatant, condescending show of arrogance, conceit, entitlement, privilege. Insult to injury.

This was the 1990s, supposedly an enlightened time, with enlightened people.

I am forty-something years old with multiple college degrees.
I am on his faculty.
I have three children.
I'm a lawyer. I'm a preacher. I'm a man.
I'm human!

But to this man birthed in privilege and nurtured in superiority I was a symbol of less than. Less than his equal. Less than a man. Subservient. Only worthy of a pat on the head.

In that moment the realization set in. Not only was everything true that I suspected about that educational environment and some of the people, but most importantly, unfortunately, I was correct in stepping away from that quicksand of dashed hopes and dreams, that cesspool of discrimination, that fairy tale of educational equality.

I should have brushed the dust from my shoes and left many years earlier. But I hadn't.

Back to the incident.

What did I do?

Just played it off, as if it didn't happen.

Stayed silent while the President continued the conversation.

I understand why victims stay quiet.

I didn't tell many people, and was careful who I told. Who would believe it?

The soft spoken huggy bear President with the ever present insincere smile and the pearly white chompers.

"Met with Dr. _____, you know what he did? After promising me a severance package? The man patted me on my head!!"

I wanted to yell, scream, push his hand away, even hit him upside his head, but I could see the headlines. They would make him a martyr, a hero. He wasn't. He isn't. His community may think so, but some of us know different.

Some know the real deal.

But after all these years I regret not saying something at that time.

Politely putting him in his place. Respectfully letting him know how wrong he was, how wrong he had been. How wrong so many of them were at that institution of higher learning.

He was the head, the leader, the face of that university.

Someone once said, "Educated fools from uneducated schools."

Day 22
Obama Wins: 2008 (Berkeley, California)

Whoops and yays, the loud cries of victory!
Like the crowd sounds at thrilling wins at a sports event.
But this was no football Super Bowl, baseball World Series or NBA seventh game championship win.
These were the neighborhood sounds I heard from my studio apartment in Berkeley, California, the night Barack Obama was elected President of the United States on the first Tuesday in November, 2008.
I lived about a block from what is known as People's Park, near the University of California's Berkeley campus. Was watching the election returns on television, like millions of others, and when the race was called, heard massive celebration in the streets.
No mistaking what I heard – shouts of joy erupting in the cool California night. Shouts from college kids? Educated folk? Liberals? African American and other ethnic groups? Who knows. I didn't go out to investigate. Didn't matter. Just a lot of very happy folk. Period.
These cheers were for the first African American President of the U.S. of A.
And yes, internally I was cheering too. Not just for the historic precedent, but for the accomplishment of this gifted, educated, visionary who believed that breaking this glass ceiling was indeed possible.
Happy for him. Happy for us. Proud.
Couldn't help but think of all those who paved the way for Mr. Obama.
Couldn't help but think of those who paid the ultimate price of their lives in the quest to exercise the right to vote.
Couldn't help but wonder what Mother, who died in 2006, would think. For years Mother would walk to the nearby neighborhood election precinct at a local church and cast her ballot. When asked who she voted for she'd always reply, "all the Democrats."

Mother voted religiously.

On the other hand, wonder what Pop would have thought about Mr. Obama. Pop was well into his 50's before he cast his first ballot. He didn't think his one vote made any difference. For years we argued and I pleaded for Pop to go cast that ballot. And Pop died in 1986.

But for whatever reason, Pop did change his mind. And Pop started taking that short walk to the neighborhood precinct to cast his ballot. I was so PROUD of him and I let him know that.

And after that first time, for either national or local elections, Pop continued to stroll that short walk and cast his ballot.

I remember clearly the first time I voted. As a freshman in college at Baker University, I walked alone to the neighborhood precinct's voting location at an elementary school. Remember thinking this was a milestone event.

It was not crowded, and I quietly and quickly cast my ballot: Jimmy Carter for President of the United States.

Fast forward twenty-eight years. Attending seminary in Berkeley I cast my ballot for Barack Obama. Waiting in eager anticipation of what might be, what might happen. What I could not have dreamed of that time when I cast my first ballot in Baldwin City, Kansas.

A golden, glorious moment.

Yep, on this November night with the heavens smiling, the moon sparkling and the stars gleaming, Mother, Pop and a great cloud of other witnesses seemed to me to be celebrating, too, joining the loud, triumphant Berkeley neighborhood chorus.

Amidst the wide smiles, hearty laughter, energetic and boisterous cheers, there were tears of immeasurable joy.

Dreams do come true! Nothing is Impossible! Hope is alive! Victory at last!

Day 23
Invisible at the Buffet: 2012-Current (Wichita, Kansas)

We are still, sometimes, invisible.

Ralph Ellison wrote about black invisibility in his 1952 novel, *Invisible Man*. Black people were invisible to society, not existing without its acknowledgement.

People (some) pretend we are not here. Not anywhere. We are not in the (their) moment.

They ignore our being, our worth. Refuse to validate us. See us as illegitimate.

For many who do see us, it is an issue of extremes. We are seen as a threat, a stereotype, an image, a caricature, less than whole. They see through their imagination.

Seems too often there is no in between. No happy medium.

It is mid-afternoon at the low cost buffet restaurant with very few customers. In fact, so few customers that some of the help are standing around talking -- to each other.

Others are on the job, taking care of business. Still others are... well, on the job but looking away from me and ignoring me.

I step over to the counter for a piece of meat to be carved. There are no other customers nearby. Might as well be in a different dimension, or so it seems. Two if not three carvers and cooks stand 10 to 15 feet away facing my direction. Don't they see me? They aren't busy cooking, grilling, cutting, stacking, sorting.

They can't help but see the space I occupy waiting for them to serve me. They just don't want to.

I wait to be served a piece of meat. The person assigned to carve it clearly sees me but leaves me standing there, plate in hand, waiting. I am being deliberately ignored.

I step away from the counter and go elsewhere to add something to my plate.

Not gone too long, just a few minutes.

Step back to the same counter. This time the restaurant manager is within a few feet, facing me talking to another employee. He sees me step to the counter for carved meat.

I look and there are still two cooks nearby, one within 10 feet. Still facing me yet she is so busy she doesn't see me. She steps to the side, yet I'm in her plain, unobstructed view.

Oh, she sees me, she knows I am there, but she chooses to play the game, the look and ignore game.

I stand there watching, waiting.

"Alana" calls her manager. He sees everything.

Instantly she is snapped back to reality. Immediately she returns from her dreamlike existence and is shuttled back into her job. Now she sees me. Back in the real world.

Not because that is her responsibility, fairness expected of staff, but because her employer commands her and she needs her wage and her job.

She scurries over and cuts a hefty piece of meat.

"Thank you" I say, thinking, *You saw me but you ignored me. You don't know me, yet you judge me. Your job is to provide service, yet until called by your supervisor you chose not to do your job when it came to serving me. Consciously or not, you played the invisible game.*

Should I have called her out? Should I have confronted her?

I chose not to. Perhaps I should have.

You see, I am black and she is brown.

Surely she knows the sting of disparate treatment, yet in this time and place she didn't care. Briefly she held the power of making the visible, invisible.

Isn't what this really is, the assertion of power over others?

And that's been a problem with humans forever.

Power, or the abuse thereof. Making visible folk, invisible. Again.

Even while trying to get a piece of meat at a buffet.

Spoils the appetite, doesn't it?

Day 24
No Discount on Grace or Store Kindness: 2012-Current (Wichita, Kansas)

After leaving the neighborhood discount retail store I got in my car but had not turned on the ignition when a Latina girl, about 10 or 11 years old, knocked on my window.
Wondered what was going on as I slowly rolled down my window.

Before I get too far ahead of myself, my trip to the store had started with an idea for hamburgers for supper, but we had no buns.
Can't have burgers without buns (well, you can use plain bread but that just wouldn't be the same. Already missing cheese and lettuce but got to have buns at least!
Off to the store for buns and a few other items I needed. The problem: had to watch my dollars (actually pennies as money was tight. Extremely tight.
Had to make choices. Had to prioritize. Had about six or seven skinny, lonely dollar bills in my wallet so I grabbed a healthy, crisp $20 bill from my emergency cache. Had not planned to spend half that much. No room to splurge.
All right, I'm good to go! I mused, ambling out the door.
Got to the store, picked up the buns, then thought of some other things.
Say, there's the over-the-counter med for that lingering, scratchy throat. Well that alone was more than $6. It would be nice to have some lettuce on the burgers, it's been awhile.
Wife likes chips but I refuse to buy a large bag, not just due to the cost but trying to cut down on calories. Will eat too many chips and feel lousy about making that choice afterward.
Decided to pick up a couple of small bags (although they nearly add up to the cost of the larger bag, but it's the principle of the thing. I had to draw the line somewhere!).
Kept looking, kept finding stuff but had to be careful.

OK, good to go. Got a few things and figured it would come up to about $15 or $16. Well, that's a bit over budget but I could deal with it.

I usually go through the self-checkout but decided this time to go through the regular checkout line.

All right, here we go! Can almost smell the burger cooking!

I watch the tally closely as the clerk rings up my groceries.

Buns, two small bags of chips, lettuce, allergy med, and another two or three small items.

Good deal! Got my buns and just a few extras!

Open my wallet and ...

Wait minute now, where is that $20? I had grabbed that $20 bill, I know I did!

One thing was for certain, it was not there!

"Sorry about that," I say to the clerk. "I left my money at home. You're going to have to void the sale."

Shucks. Look at my items, all that time and trouble trying to be careful about what I picked up. Paying very close attention to the price labels.

OK, what do we really need for dinner? Don't have to put e-v-e-r-y-t-h-i-n-g back. Buns, got to have the buns!

I look at how many singles I have. Don't want to spend everything. Clerk asked how much I have. I reply in a round figure but not the exact amount. Don't want to be broke, even if it is only for a few minutes till I get home. Anything, as I can clearly see, can happen.

"Please put back the ..."

I start telling the clerk what items to take off the bill, to put back on the shelves, to... Well, you get the picture. No choice, I'm leaving most of my groceries. Period.

"Sorry for the inconvenience," I tell the very patient and understanding clerk. "Sorry for holding up the line." Although before there wasn't much of a queue, there is now. Bunch of folks with a bunch of stuff.

"That's all right," offers the sympathetic, thirty-something clerk, a man who has undoubtedly seen this before. But, as for me... I've never, ever done that before, gone off and left my money somewhere.

In my wallet there is very little money on either bank card. A small limit credit card hides in a dark, tightly closed closet at home, accompanied by mostly dated clothing.

Finally, I pay for the buns and I leave my forsaken meds, chips, lettuce at the register.

I grab my small bag and slowly trudge toward my dented and dinged, Old Blue, a small, elderly, compact, two-door that started as our second son's college car in New Orleans, then became our first son's graduate school car in Connecticut, then our only daughter's high school car in Iowa, and now served as our family car in Kansas. The car, like us, has been around more than one block.

On through the parking lot I walk, slow, agonizing. What a way to live! Surviving, day to day, moment to moment.

"This too shall pass," is the sentiment that usually provides solace. On this day, however, that provides very little comfort.

I get to the car, open the door and slide under the steering wheel, tossing the bag with the buns on the front passenger seat.

There's a knock on my car window.

What's going on here? I wonder. Don't know the young Latina girl, have not seen her before.

"Tap, tap, tap." She softly strikes my window. I gaze at her face. I see anticipation and excitement in her eyes.

"Sir, we wanted to give you this," and she hands me the bag full of the groceries I'd just left in the store.

I am shocked, amazed at this sudden, gracious act of kindness! Sincerely moved. This has never happened before! What a day!

I thank God, not only for the groceries but for this act of kindness, the reminder that there are still those people who show compassion, understanding and empathy to others, even strangers. People who care for others and cross color, cultural, economic, social, religious, ethnic, political, racial, age, gender, and all other human-constructed lines.

I will pray for this girl and her family, for this is indeed an exercise of unconditional love. Thinking of me. Seeing me. Taking action.

Discount retail groceries, perhaps, but no discount on grace.

"Thank you, thank you very much," I stammer to my young Angel. Mission accomplished, Grace smiles, turns and sprints away.

Day 25
Mr. Walmart Greeter: 2012-Current (Wichita, Kansas)

Hey Mr. Walmart Greeter!
Dressed in your blue store sanctioned vest, standing guard in the grand entrance of the retail castle, your dark, suspicious eyes and penetrating gaze meet me as I enter your fiefdom. Stringy, fine black hair, caramel colored skin, a fellow person of color. I expected more from you.
Of course I should have known better by now. While we had gender, height and middle age in common, the fact that we shared some type of minority heritage meant absolutely nothing.
His eyes told his story.
Despite his j – o – b. That is, supposedly, to "greet" customers of Walmart.
Yet his only greeting was a look of disdain, skepticism, judgment.
His eyes made clear what his voice dared not utter.
And I made my way past his misguided, warped perception.
But you are paid to Greet!
Oh, I forgot, that is to greet certain people.
I strolled this economic plantation, completed my task, found my commodities, and exchanged currency for my purchases. And I exited the same way I entered, passing his invisible security moat.
What is this????!!!!
"Thank you for shopping at Walmart!"
My ears are finally soothed by his enthusiastic voice expressing seemingly sincere gratitude for my afternoon shopping experience.
Oh, no! His flowery mask of plastic appreciation was not tendered for my ears! It was directed toward lighter, apparently brighter ears belonging to the Caucasian couple a few steps in front of me. I felt like a jilted, scorned suitor.
Again his beady, steely eyes met mine as I walked past him. His voice remained stone silent.

Seconds later I heard his booming voice of grand appreciation. "Thank you for shopping at Walmart!" directed to another Caucasian couple just a few steps behind me.

Mr. Walmart-Greeter: Your preference is crystal clear. Certain people are most welcome in your kingdom. Certain people and their money are preferred.

Doesn't my money spend just like theirs?

In fact, my money makes YOUR money POSSIBLE.

Day 26
Oil Change and Price Check: 2012-Current (Wichita, Kansas)

How long does it take to answer the question, "How much is an oil and filter change?"

In the case of one Wichita oil change service facility, for me, more than twenty minutes.

For someone else, a matter of seconds.

Some things, being African American, living black in the U.S. of A., you just f-e-e-l, you know. You feel prejudice.

The twenty-minute price check story goes like this...

An oil change was long overdue. Severe cold weather was sneaking into our area and I needed an oil change like yesterday. Didn't want to go back to the oil change facility we had frequented for the last few years because of another sorry experience of lousy customer service. I decided to go to Jiffy Lube. We'd utilized them before and I should have known better.

I had a coupon which indicated the oil filter change was "$21.99 up to $22 off" the usual oil change price. But "off" what?

I phoned, mentioned the coupon and was told a price of $25 and some odd cents.

The service attendant added that it depended upon the oil "package" selected.

OK, so there are apparently, choices.

Within 15 to 20 minutes I pull into the Jiffy Lube location I'd called, exit my vehicle and enter the waiting room.

One other customer, a twenty-something Caucasian female sits comfortably, waiting.

The service advisor greets me, and I state my interest in an oil change and ask the price of the oil and filter change, mentioning the coupon.

The rangy, beady-eyed, middle-aged Caucasian service advisor does not look at the coupon or answer my question. He mumbles,

"There's a customer in front of you. Soon as I finish with her and get you pulled into the garage I'll go over all of that with you. Are the keys in the car?"

I hesitate, fearing once the car is in the garage I will incur some additional charge.

But what kind of business technique is this? What does this man think I am? I know what's going on here and why. Start to walk out and go elsewhere. But I really needed an oil change, so I relent and hand over the keys.

Watch the car pull in. Watch the workers finish the female customer's vehicle.

Watch the employees start servicing my car, vacuuming, raising the hood, checking fluids, checking the VIN number, all without answering my preliminary question of "how much?"

Several minutes pass and the same service advisor asks for an update on my personal information (it had been two or three years since the last visit. Finally he states:

"Let me see your coupon."

He continues with the computer screen; I quickly see several oil change packages flicker by. Without clarification he makes a selection, still without offering comments about what's available, why and how much.

He finishes and declares, "We'll get you taken care of." He turns to walk away.

But still nothing about price?

"Hey, you haven't said anything about what the price will be?" I inquire.

He turns on a dime and snaps:

"$21.99 plus tax, that is what the coupon says doesn't it?"

I am shocked at his patronizing tone and condescending, snotty attitude. He must be confused; I am the customer here. Oh, that's right, he sees only a black man.

I don't argue as that was what the coupon said and was in line with what the prior service tech told me on the phone.

No need to raise my blood pressure at this time and place.

So I let it go. I finally get the price check, after a wait while the car is vacuumed, fluids checked, and the preliminary inspection of the car completed.

A few minutes later the same service advisor presents me with a sheet on which he has chicken scratched some areas of the car that need attention, i.e., oil and filter change, busted windshield wiper blade, radiator flush, etc. He presents his estimate: $250.

Really? Apparently I looked like a customer who would buy a New York city bridge!

I ask the price of just the radiator flush. He mumbles something about $180 to $190 but he can bring it down to $160. As I look at the figures he then adds, "I can bring that down to $116 today."

A big decrease from that $250 bargain he first quoted.

"No thank you, just the oil and filter change today."

He stresses the need of the radiator flush as the Freon registers only about ten degrees above and he warns to have it done or "it will freeze."

How thoughtful.

They finish, I pay and leave. But feel like I need a shower.

The service advisor thinks that's the end, it isn't.

I write letters of complaint. To the corporate president. To the Better Business Bureau.

The service advisor has to be called on his judging a book by its cover. Making assumptions that I could be taken in. Hopefully he got the message.

Next time, just answer the simple question: "How much does it cost?" That shouldn't depend on the customer's color, culture, religion, or sex. Shouldn't be randomly adjusted, whether paid with cash, check, credit or debit card, or money order. The bottom line is it should be simple: Just give the price. That's all.

Dollars and cents.

Keep it that way.

Day 27
Voting Rights: 2021 (Wichita, Kansas)

Voting – the power to choose. Where a usually nondescript, over shadowed people's voices can sing, loud and powerfully. Voting -- the basic right of Americans, admired across the world.

People, of all colors, including many black folk, died to exercise this right. But this very basic, fundamental core of democracy, is being peeled away like the skin off an apple, layer by layer like the insides of an onion. Do you see it?

Since the 2020 Presidential election of Democrats Joe Biden and Kamala Harris, Republican-led state legislatures across the country have enacted bill after bill making it harder to vote. Sanctions, prohibitions and penalties in new state laws are supposedly designed to discourage fraud in voting, despite no credible evidence of voting fraud in 2020, as the courts have repeatedly found.

The only fraudulent behavior is that manifested by the Republicans. They know what they are doing and why they do it. We all know: Voter suppression.

Although the methodology of voter suppression has changed since the 1960s and 1970s, the overall impact remains the same. Make early voting more difficult and ban others from assisting those who are disabled or without transport. Ban providing voters water as they wait in line to vote. Threaten nonpartisan groups with felony charges for registering or assisting voters. This is how state legislatures are legislating disenfranchisement. And because of the growing number of voters of color, such legislation legalizes institutional racism.

Legislators with hard, cold eyes and nerves of steel enact these laws dressed in fashionable expensive suits or dresses.

Just like before. Many times before. After Reconstruction. During Jim Crow. The federal Voting Rights Act of 1965 protected voters from state laws disenfranchising them. Now, with the Voting Rights

Act of 1965 gradually weakened and no new federal law, some states are back to disenfranchising.

And just like before, they expect us to believe they mean well, to accept their rhetoric and their version of the truth. Words like belief and truth are so intangible, so subjective, so open to interpretation.

They claim to believe, as they've been told by President #45, that the presidential election of 2020 was stolen, that there was massive fraud, that #45 actually won.

They claim the election numbers lie.

These politicians claim to believe this version of the truth and are doing everything to reconstruct the system to ensure that next time around the results will be different. That their claim of electoral victory will become the actual truth next time. Of course, with a little help from invention, concoction, deception, and lies.

Thought there was a commandment in the Bible about lying. One of those "shall nots." Must be mistaken.

Day 28
Utility Poles: 2017-Current (Wichita, Kansas)

Never thought a utility pole could speak.
Say what?
Like reflecting how some folks are viewed by others. Like manifesting bias, prejudice, and bigotry. Institutionally. Systemic. racism. And let's not forget class.

Utility poles are raised on city street corners or intersecting alleys in certain neighborhoods. Note the word "certain." These monstrosities are erected under the ruse of community benefit but actually to maximize utility companies' profits.

I see a towering gray needle of steel loudly proclaiming a reminder that some of us, inhabitants of the northeast of Wichita, Kansas, are viewed as less than, "the other" and "those people." This lower income neighborhood, which decades ago was predominantly African American, is a mixture of all kinds of colors and ethnic groups including Caucasian, Hispanic, African American, and others. Growing up on this block in the 1960s and 1970s it was only black folk.

Growing up at that time on my street, down the very next block lived Wichita's first black mayor, A. Price Woodard, Jr. Often I would see him walk the sidewalk in front of my house. Nice man who would always speak. I wonder what he would say about this neighborhood change and the gigantic steel reminders of our status in some folks' eyes. Views about and toward us.

As mentioned, all kinds of things have changed in this neighborhood where I grew up. And the influx of all kinds of different folk, and that's a good thing.

But some things have not changed. And the actions of the utility company serve as a stark reminder of that.

On the northeast side of town, a traditionally lower income and predominantly black neighborhood, the utility company places these huge utility poles that are twice the size of the usual wooden poles.

The poles go up without notifying many neighborhood residents impacted by this imposition.

As reported by Chance Swaim in his article in *The Wichita Eagle*, "Gov. Kelly touts new power-pole transparency law." In 2018 the Evergy utility company constructed 105-foot-tall steel poles in the Black, low income neighborhood to support high voltage lines connecting three substations -- without informing residents or the city of their plans. State government officials enacted a law that required more transparency from utility companies. However, the bottom line is the law does not require utility companies to obtain government approval of such plans.

Now my house is located on a lot adjacent to a property housing one such pole. If by negligence or act of God – e.g., earthquake -- that pole was to fall, it could not only hit but destroy my house.

Yep, it's that close.

There was an outcry from many residents, backed by some city and state officials, blasting the arrogance and conceit of the utility company. Some city officials claimed they did not have advance notice of the scheme nor any authority to stop the utility company.

Say what?

And the utility agreed to move or reduce the height of some of the towers in northeast Wichita. Just not the one outside my door. Not the dozen or so others that line 11th Street for several blocks in my neighborhood. The utility company also offered to make other provisions to impacted residents to calm the raging outcry. For example, the utility tried to make nice by offering a few dollars for neighborhood improvement that would benefit a few residents. Note: only some folks received the offer.

Nothing offered regarding the resulting decrease in property values. Little said about the defacement and mutilation of the neighborhood's aesthetics. Evergy said little regarding how the decision was reached to inflict those towering examples of marginalization only on this particular area.

I've only seen one other utility pole like those in my neighborhood. Only one. In a neighboring county, near a two lane highway, in a rural area with nary a house in sight.

But we have a whole bunch. It is all hunky dory and business as usual. We know where we stand. The attitude is unmistakable, the language is clear, the words are precise: the utility poles have spoken.

Day 29
Death of a Friendship: 2020-21 (Wichita, Kansas)

It was painful and I struggled with the decision for months. But it was time to let the longtime, nearly 50-year friendship die.

Politics mixed with racism, class, and perhaps some other isms, (age, sex, etc. with a dash of pride and a pinch of stubborn narrowmindedness drove us apart.

Far apart. Over Ideology, Philosophy, Theology -- Everything.

We met in junior high school. He was Caucasian, lived on the opposite side of town in a lower middle-class neighborhood and was a staunch Republican, even though we were too young to vote.

Didn't matter. We met in some type of shop class, perhaps woodworking or metals. We were classmates and shared a mutual friend. And in time we became friends. We were more alike than different: we loved sports, especially basketball, talking about girls and having a good time. Nothing particularly dangerous or illegal, just doing what young people during the 1970s did.

Most of all, we laughed. He had quite a sense of humor and we enjoyed each other's company.

However, even then he would say or do something I found offensive or disrespectful and I'd chide him about it. It was not racial or stereotypical but sometimes his opinionated attitude or observations would grate on folk. Some just didn't care for him, and they'd let me know. He could never understand why, even then.

There were times when he would cross the line and I'd have to put time and space between us. Perhaps he knew why, maybe not. And that "time" could last for years.

We'd eventually resume contact, get caught up, and act as if nothing ever happened.

Yes, we were friends. Close friends. Best of friends. From junior high through high school, college, and young adulthood (when I left Wichita and he started his career of establishing many different small but successful businesses.

Our friendship endured. Across the miles, across time. Through major and minor events: marriages, children, bankruptcies, financial problems, successes, and deaths. From politicians and presidents to apartments, townhouses and homes. He remained in Wichita while I lived here and there.

All through the years he remained a conservative Republican (with the exception of 2008 when he admitted to voting for Barack Obama and I always remained a liberal Democrat.

What happened?

Somewhere along the line what started as a minor crack in the connection became more, much more. Attitudes, observations, opinions which were once forgettable and forgivable became ... let's say unacceptable to me, almost obscene.

His views of "others" different from him became more pronounced, more extreme, and more radical. Little to no concern for the oppressed, the marginalized, the abused, the stereotyped, the disenfranchised. Little to no regard for people like me.

We once -- outside of his upper middle-class brick home with its well-manicured yard -- had a discussion about racism and discrimination while he tinkered with the electronics of his brand new vehicle. I told him about a few of my experiences of less than fair and equal treatment in Wichita. He couldn't understand. He couldn't empathize. Why? Because he hadn't seen or experienced it.

Of course not. But the trouble was, he didn't want to see it.

I was disturbed by his attitude.

He continued to travel down the road of extremism and radicalism. Posted and reposted offensive, derogatory racial comments and memes on his Facebook page. We had been friends, for years. But now he sank into a world of disbelief, manipulation, bias, and prejudice. Against others different from him by race, culture, economics, politics, social standing, class, country of origin, sexual orientation.

Donald Trump his proud President. My once close friend viewed Trump as king and, yes, even granted him godlike status.

The straw that broke the camel's back was his reposting of a comment that I'll paraphrase: "There was a racist in the White House, but we got rid of him." Posted there was a photograph of Obama.

Eventually I stopped making much contact with my old friend. Communication dwindled to about once a year. He would still call on or near my birthday and if I missed his annual call, I returned his yearly greetings. Yes, he remembered my birthday. That once a year contact continued for a handful of years. Sometimes he mentioned that he wondered why he didn't hear from me. I said something like I realized how busy he was and left it at that.

Many times I'd call, leave messages, and never hear from him. When we'd chat I'd suggest getting together for lunch or something, but the time was never right. Sometimes he'd mentioned having the wife and me over for dinner, but it never happened. We were both making excuses. You get the picture.

The final phone call came in April 2020, during the early stages of the COVID-19 pandemic. We chatted, as usual. He was going to contact me again in the summer. Didn't happen. I was fine if it happened, fine if it didn't.

People come. People go. There are friends for a reason, and friends for a season.

The season for this friendship had run its course. Early the following year, I received word that my longtime friend had died suddenly. I was saddened. Remembered the good old times. The wonderful times. The highlights. But he was gone, forever. The friendship had survived for nearly 50 years, but now it was over. It had died long ago.

Day 30
Reading & Places: Travel Real and Imagined

Long as I can remember I have loved reading.

It started with Mother reading to me as a little boy, and I became anxious to learn to read for myself.

I was not bound by any limits when reading, enjoying reading a cacophony of human experiences and emotions all wrapped up in words.

Reading opens the mind to previously unknown possibilities. You can even become someone else and see, hear, smell through the senses of a character.

Reading can lead to personal change. Transformation.

Reading provides fuel for today's hopes and tomorrow's dreams.

Mother knew the power of words. There was always something to read around the house. And Mother taught by modeling, beginning with a Bible and a Sunday School book on the nightstand next to her bed. Many a night I remember her sitting on the side of her bed, glasses resting on her nose, reading.

And she planted the seeds of reading early. When I was a small child, often she would go to the store and return with one of those children's Golden Books. It wasn't long before I had quite a collection of Golden Books safely stored in the drawer of a living room table. They were my pride and joy. And I had a huge Bible stories book for children with bright, colorful pictures that I loved.

The seed was nurtured and I realized early the joys of reading. I could travel to faraway, exotic places, relive historical events, meet people who changed the world!

Years later I was able to go to some of the places I first visited in books.

For example, in the fall of 1977 when I first ventured to DC as a transfer student at American University and stepped foot in the White House during a public tour. This was before cement barriers, metal detectors and terrorism became words in our lexicon. Walking in the home of Presidents, enveloped with the fragrance of the past while immersed in the sunlight of the present, my eyes couldn't believe what they were seeing. What a place! Never forgot that feeling.

And I have visited many other fascinating places including but not limited to: the beautiful, rolling hills of Scotland; the peaceful, comfortable English countryside; the Eiffel Tower, Buckingham Palace, and the Roman Colosseum; Mt. Stanserhorn in Switzerland.

The most moving was my first trip abroad when I visited the Holy Land, Israel and Jordan, actually seeing many places I'd first seen in my old King James Bible. The traditional Mt. Nebo and the magnificent, beautiful red walls of Petra in Jordan. A glass bottom boat ride on the Red Sea, and another boat trip on the Sea of Galilee. Inside the tomb of Lazarus where I bumped my head exiting.

But even more. Baptism in Yardenit in the River Jordan, walking in the Garden of Gethsemane, standing inside the Church of the Nativity in Bethlehem, the landmark that commemorates the place of Jesus' birth.

I have been inside two places that mark the death and resurrection of Jesus, The Church of the Holy Sepulcher and The Garden Tomb. I was inside the tomb(s) of Jesus, the traditional Orthodox, Roman Catholic, and Protestant sites of his tombs.

This is not the place for sophisticated debate over the legitimacy of the present structures and the like.

The key point is, this place is the location, the environment, where many of those Biblical events happened. These places became real because of books, pictures, photographs, and words.

The power of words.
The power of dreams.
The power of reading.
Read on, children. Read on. And dream.
And thank you Mother. Across eternity.
With Love.

Day 31
Hope: 2012-Current (Wichita, Kansas)

"Keep Hope Alive!"

Many years ago when the Rev. Jesse Jackson uttered that rallying cry it really didn't resonate with me. Of course, I understood the meaning as well as why he was issuing that emotional mandate. Without hope, dreams die. Without hope, the spirit languishes and when hopelessness sets in, there's danger.

I have been through several gut-wrenching trials in this life.

I know what it is like to barely keep my head above water, what it's like to nearly drown in seemingly "hopeless" situations.

Thus I was well acquainted with the importance of remembering that the sun continues to shine despite the thick, bleak, sometimes ominous black clouds of life that hide it.

And in 2008 when Mr. Barack Obama ran his first U.S. Presidential campaign on the theme of "hope," and made history in our time, that was more evidence that, in time, the bright light of Hope continues to shine. That was something that I believed in 100 per cent, but I always tied hope together with faith.

His victory nourished my hope despite the seemingly impossible conditions of the economic crisis.

I was a staunch supporter of Mr. Obama before, during and after his White House years.

As my years mount up, however, life's darts, daggers and disappointments continue to stretch my faith and test the boundaries of my hope. Then toss in the warring battle with the flesh and, unfortunately, add Evil.

Now mix in those innermost complex, fluid emotions and reactions to life's arrows and snares and one can easily fall into despair, frustration, loneliness, fatigue, and the suffocating pit of negativity.

One can also become callous and oblivious to the beauty and wonder of this world, its freshness and vibrancy. Can be overshadowed by the putrid smell of injustice, oppression, abuse, and unfairness -- you know, racism, sexism, ageism, what groups of humans use to distinguish themselves from others.

I understand how some give in, give up and give out.

I understand how some can relegate themselves to seemingly self-isolated bubbles and refuse to come out.

And that's where hope comes in.

One thing about hitting rock bottom, you know it. Flat on your mental, emotional and spiritual back, you missed that right jab or the left upper cut that perhaps blindsided you and left you reeling. Maybe you even saw it coming but didn't duck it in time, or thought you could withstand the blow.

Anyway, you're flat on your back from an apparent, surefire knockout punch. Down. And the enemy, whoever it may be, in whatever form, is trying to count you out.

Six…seven…eight…

But reach up, out, and for hope!

Look deep within yourself for that spark of hope and then, keep focused. Don't take your sight off of it. Move toward it, whatever that may mean, wherever it takes you.

Remember prior times and victories won.

Remember highpoints and highlights.

Remember those mountaintop moments.

And realize achievement, success, and victory can happen again.

Know that you are indeed special and have something to contribute.

Do whatever is necessary to grab and hold onto hope for dear life.

Hope again.

Hope for a new thing.

Hope for a better day.

Hope for a change.

Hope for a difference.

Hope for…

Hope in…

Sometimes hope's light will shine through God's creation, the majesty and brilliance of this world. Of creatures. Like the wonder of a flaming, bright red Cardinal. Or the grace of the floating, light-as-a-feather Monarch butterfly. The joyful, playful antics of a puppy. The gleaming, sparkling eyes and bright, wide grin of a toddler. The fresh, cool air of an ocean breeze.

Sometimes hope may come through another person. Spouse, lover, family, friend, acquaintance, even a stranger.

Sometimes it may come through a situation, an event, an activity.

Sometimes it may come from deep within your soul, the awakening of the spirit to the voice of love, the God of eternity. The resurrected Jesus ascending, promising to be with us until the end age, which means in every situation or circumstance. Forever.

Regardless of how it comes, it will come, so sink your teeth into it, holding on like a dog with a bone.

Embrace it. Again.

And if indeed it is lost, seek and find it again.

Life depends upon it. Your life.

The End

About the Author

Reginald D. Jarrell has taught at St. Ambrose University, Davenport, Iowa; Southern University in New Orleans, Louisiana; and Alcorn State University, Lorman, Mississippi; as well as at two community colleges in Iowa and Illinois. His legal experience includes work as an assistant public defender, Rock Island County, Illinois, and staff attorney, Prairie State Legal Services, Rock Island. His communications experience includes working as television production staff, Family Radio, Oakland, California; as a newspaper staff reporter for The Moline Publishing Company, Moline, Illinois; and as a television news reporter, WHO-TV, Des Moines, Iowa. He has also worked as a janitor and a shoe salesperson.

He earned a Juris Doctor degree, University of Iowa College of Law, Iowa City, Iowa; a Master of Divinity, American Baptist Seminary of the West, Berkeley, California; a Master of Science, Mass Communication and Journalism, Iowa State University, Ames, Iowa; a Bachelor of Arts in Communication, The American University, Washington, D.C.; and is completing a Doctor of Ministry degree from The Berkeley School of Theology, formerly American Baptist Seminary of the West.

Jarrell's writing includes essays, memoirs, children's books and television/film screenplays. He enjoys reading, film, theater, travel and current events.

Jarrell's family consists of wife Canetha, two sons, one daughter, six grandchildren, and one small dog. Jarrell has lived in several places across the United States and currently resides in south central Kansas.

www.ingramcontent.com/pod-product-compliance
Lightning Source LLC
Chambersburg PA
CBHW070046120526
44589CB00035B/2358